Key For Two

CW00551165

A Comedy

John Chapman
and
Dave Freeman

•

Samuel French – London
New York – Sydney – Toronto – Hollywood

Please see page 64 for further copyright information

KEY FOR TWO

First presented at the Vaudeville Theatre, London, by Duncan C. Weldon with Paul Gregg and Lionel Becker for Triumph Apollo Productions and Pieter Toerien on 8th September 1982, with the following cast of characters:

Gordon	Patrick Cargill
Harriet	Moira Lister
Alec	Glyn Houston
Anne	Barbara Murray
Richard	David Stoll
Magda	Sonia Graham
Mildred	Eileen Anson

Directed by Dennis Ramsden

Designed by John Page

The action of the play takes place in the sitting-room and bedroom of Harriet's Regency flat in Brighton

ACT I
 SCENE 1 Monday morning
 SCENE 2 Some time later
 SCENE 3 Wednesday afternoon

ACT II Later that night

Time — the present

Photograph by Stuart Anderson

ACT I

SCENE 1

The sitting-room and bedroom of Harriet's elegant Regency flat in Brighton. Monday morning

Most of the stage is occupied by the sitting-room. About a third is given over to a small bedroom UR, with a double bed, a small gilt wicker chair, a chest of drawers and a bedside table. The bedroom section is on a raised dais. In the back wall upstage of the bed there is a window and L, set at right angles to the back wall, there is a door which leads from the sitting-room into the bedroom. Another door UR leads into the bathroom. The wall around the bedroom is imagined and the rest of the stage below the bedroom is part of the sitting-room. DR there is a door into the dining-room and there is also a door DL going to the kitchen. UCL there is an archway leading to the hall which has a front door R and a spare bedroom to L. The furnishings in the sitting-room are elegant and in the style of the house. There are two chairs, a small sofa, a writing-desk and chair, and a sofa table which has a shelf underneath for drinks

When the CURTAIN rises, Gordon is putting on his tie in the bedroom. Gordon is in his forties, handsome, athletic and runs a successful advertising agency. He is dressed in trousers and shirt and his jacket is over the wicker chair

Harriet enters from the kitchen carrying a breakfast tray and goes into the bedroom. She is a very glamorous woman of about forty and will probably continue looking forty for years to come. She is intensely feminine and fun. She wears a gorgeous housecoat over her nightie

Harriet Oh, you're up, I thought we'd have breakfast in bed.
Gordon Oh, sorry.

Gordon has coffee and toast as he finishes dressing. Harriet looks out of the window and then sits on the bed with the tray

Harriet That garden fence is nearly down. Look at it.
Gordon Haven't time at the moment. Can't you get someone in to mend it?
Harriet It's not that, darling, it's the cost of everything. Everyone wants the earth. The Gas Board have sent us a bill for twenty-seven pounds for mending the water heater and the man was only here three minutes.
Gordon Well, query it. You can query it you know.
Harriet I wanted to tie them up today.
Gordon Tie who up?
Harriet The roses, they're sprawling all over the place.
Gordon Well tie them up, then.
Harriet I can't with the fence half down.

Gordon This coffee tastes off.

Harriet No, the coffee's all right, it's the milk that's off.

Gordon Yes, you're right.

Harriet It's that fridge, it's not working properly.

Gordon Nothing in this place is working properly. The water heater, the fence, the fridge. It's all crumbling about our ears.

Harriet I know, darling, I do the best I can.

Gordon Harriet, I can't let you have any more money. I just don't have it.

Harriet I didn't ask for any, darling. I mean, I'm not the one who's complaining, I'm drinking *my* coffee. (*She sips her coffee and grimaces*)

Gordon I shouldn't bother.

Harriet I'm trying to save money.

Gordon Harriet, I give you a hell of a whack every month to keep this place going, but business is awful at the moment. God knows what we're going to learn today at the board meeting.

Harriet Oh you'll be splendid, darling. You'll bring them all round to your way of thinking.

Gordon That won't be difficult . . . we all think the same way . . . how to avoid going bankrupt.

Harriet Oh, it can't be as bad as that.

Gordon It's a world wide recession, Harriet, and our advertising agency hasn't a single safe account left.

Gordon strides out of the bedroom into the sitting-room and goes to the desk. Harriet picks up the tray and follows him. He opens his briefcase and starts going through some papers. Harriet goes towards the kitchen with the tray

We're facing complete financial disaster.

Harriet It's not an awfully good moment, but you haven't given me the housekeeping yet.

Harriet exits to the kitchen

Gordon Yes, all right. (*He sits as he takes out his cheque book and pen*)

Harriet (*off*) A couple of extra bills came yesterday, darling, they're on the desk.

Gordon picks up the bills and looks at the first one. He groans

Gordon Oh, it's awful. (*He looks at the second bill and groans again*) Oh, my God!

Harriet (*off*) I didn't show them to you last night . . . I didn't want to ruin your evening.

Gordon Well it hasn't helped the morning much. (*He starts to write the cheque and stops*) I don't even give my wife this much.

Harriet enters with a vase of flowers which she puts on the sofa table

Harriet What, darling?

Gordon Oh, nothing.

Harriet I thought you said something about your wife.

Gordon Yes, I've had to cut down on her housekeeping.

Harriet Oh, Gordon, poor woman. How on earth can she manage?

Gordon She seems to cope. Mind you the meals are getting a bit ropey. Thank God I'm not often at home.

Harriet If you didn't waste money on women, you'd have more to spend on your wife.

Gordon That I find rather odd, coming from you.

Harriet Don't evade the issue. You've no sense of responsibility.

Gordon Don't nag me, Harriet. I get quite enough of that at home.

Harriet Sorry, I didn't mean to hen-peck.

Gordon Oh hens, that reminds me. I'll bring you some more eggs.

Harriet Darling, I could feed Africa on the eggs you bring. Couldn't you manage the odd chicken once in a while?

Gordon (*shocked*) Good God, no. That would be like breaking into capital.

Harriet How many do you have?

Gordon Well let me see ... there's Emily, Marigold, Fiona, Penelope ... and of course, Fred.

Harriet Well you wouldn't miss Fred, would you?

Gordon No, but they would. Anyway you said you liked eggs.

Harriet Oh, I do ... in moderation.

Gordon (*getting up*) Well, I prefer them to all that fish you keep serving up. (*He shuts his briefcase and puts it by the hall table*)

Harriet I thought you liked fish.

Gordon Well yes, once in a while, but not the vast quantities we seem to consume. It must cost a fortune.

Harriet I don't pay for it. Mummy brings it.

Gordon Well let her eat it. I'd like a change sometimes.

Harriet All right, what would you like for dinner on Wednesday?

Gordon You mean Friday. Wednesday's Magda's birthday, I can't miss that.

Harriet No, of course not. I'm sorry I meant Friday. What can I tickle your fancy with?

Gordon Ah, well could we have those lamb chops done in cider?

Harriet Yes, all right.

Gordon And could you copy out that recipe for Magda ... ?

Harriet What, *now*?

Gordon It's pretty urgent. The meal she served up on Monday was appalling. God knows what she'd done to it. Go on, jot it down.

Harriet I thought you were pushed for time ...

Gordon No ...

Harriet sits at the desk and starts to jot down the recipe

(*Looking at the clock*) Wait a minute, is that clock right?

Harriet Yes, to the second.

Gordon (*looking at his watch*) Well I'm fast ... (*He presses the button of the watch*) Oh hell, I was on Johannesburg time. It keeps slipping from one time to another. I have to look at Johannesburg and subtract two hours. It won't stop on Greenwich ... Oh that's that last damned straw ... That's the end. (*He takes off his watch*)

Harriet (*scribbling*) Don't make such a fuss, it's not a catastrophe.

Gordon It's our account. We have to sell the damn things and all I can get is Johannesburg ... Haven't you seen our slogan, "The Watch of the Future

as worn by Astronauts'"? (*He holds his watch by the strap and bangs it on his wrist*) Bloody thing!
Harriet I'm sure they'll be all right as long as they all splash down in Johannesburg.
Gordon She's doing Hungarian Goulash tonight. That could mean anything.
Harriet Oh, nonsense.
Gordon Have you thought any more about it?
Harriet What?
Gordon My leaving her and coming in with you.
Harriet No, thank you.
Gordon But, Harriet.
Harriet I've had one husband and that's quite enough.
Gordon Yes, but he was a rotten double-dealing swine with a bit on the side.
Harriet Yes ... ?
Gordon Yes, well ... I mean ... I know ... but we're different, I love you.
Harriet And I love you, too, so let's not spoil it by getting married. Now, here's your recipe.

Harriet stands up and hands Gordon the recipe and he tucks it into his breast pocket, then he grabs her

Gordon If you won't marry me, why can't I move in with you?
Harriet I'm afraid Mummy wouldn't take too kindly to our little set up.
Gordon Perhaps if I could meet her ...
Harriet No, Gordon. She's rather old fashioned, even prudish.
Gordon She doesn't seem too prudish when it comes to the question of drink. By the look of those bills she's marinated in vodka.
Harriet She enjoys a little drink sometimes.
Gordon Yes, but it's my little drink, isn't it?
Harriet Sometimes she brings a friend or two.
Gordon Pretty thirsty ones. I mean I don't mind buying it for us, but I can't afford to supply the neighbourhood.
Harriet I'll have a word with her.
Gordon What happens if she asks to come on one of my days?
Harriet I simply tell her I'm working.
Gordon As what?
Harriet A private secretary to a very demanding gentleman who requires a twenty-four hour a day service when called for.

He draws her to him

Gordon Oh that perfume ... what is it?
Harriet It's a quarter-past eight.
Gordon Masses of time. Let's go back to bed.
Harriet And what about this board meeting ... ?
Gordon I'll ring them later and tell them I've been held up.
Harriet How much later?

They go to the bedroom

Gordon That depends on you.

Harriet I know you, you'll go off to sleep again.
Gordon I'll set the alarm. (*He fiddles with his watch*)
Harriet But that watch is wrong. (*She takes her housecoat off and hangs it on the hook on the bedroom door*)
Gordon I'll set the alarm clock, that goes off like a fire gong.

Harriet slips under the bed covers and he starts to undress speedily as —

the CURTAIN *falls*

Immediately a loud alarm clock rings

SCENE 2

The same. Sometime later

The alarm clock is still ringing as the CURTAIN *rises after a few seconds*

Harriet sits up, stretches out an arm and turns off alarm clock. Then she shakes the sleeping figure next to her, hidden under the bedclothes

Harriet Darling... Darling... Wake up... You'll be late. I told you you'd go off to sleep again.

A figure sits up. It is Alec. He is a North-country man, in his fifties, big, bluff and owns a fleet of trawlers

Alec Oh, hell. What time is it?
Harriet Well look. It's nearly ten.
Alec Oh, that's not too bad.
Harriet What do you want for breakfast?
Alec No breakfast. I'm on a diet, remember?
Harriet Yes, of course, darling. I've got a memory like a sieve.
Alec I've noticed that. Still, the rest of you's all right. Give us a kiss.
Harriet Yes, all right, but I want some breakfast even if you don't.
Alec Come on.
Harriet Oh, why do you all get so amorous in the mornings?
Alec What do you mean ... you all?
Harriet Oh, it's a thing I picked up off Mummy. She lived for years in Alabama ... you know ... (*with an accent*) yo all.
Alec I'd like to meet this mother of yours one day. She's travelled a lot, hasn't she? (*He gets out of bed*)
Harriet Yes. Oh, darling, before I forget, that garden fence is nearly down. Shall I get someone in to do it?
Alec (*glancing through the window*) No, they charge the earth. That'll cost you about a hundred and fifty quid. I'll have a go at it next time I come down.
Harriet That's what you all say ... (*Hastily*) You always say.
Alec I'll do it. It won't take me long. Didn't I buy the nails for it?
Harriet No.
Alec No, you're right ... those were for mending the trellis at home.
Harriet They must have been.

Alec I'll bring some of them down. They're a hell of a price now, nails. I'll have to finish that trellis first though. Mildred's nagging the life out of me. All her roses are dangling over the path.
Harriet So are mine. I thought you had a gardener?
Alec We did have. He's packed the job in. Gone in for demolition. He should do very well. He's had enough practice on our place.

Alec exits to the bathroom

The phone rings. Harriet picks it up

Harriet Hello? Five-five-o-two-one. . . . Gordon! (*She looks towards the bathroom. Speaking in a low voice*) Can you ring back later? Mummy's here.
Alec (*off*) Who is it?
Harriet It's Gor——Mummy.
Alec Who?
Harriet (*cupping the phone*) Poor Mummy. (*Into the phone*) Just hold on. (*She puts the phone under the pillow and goes to the bathroom door*) I'll just close the door, darling, in case she can hear the shower. (*She closes the bathroom door and returns to the phone*) It's all right, Gordon, Mummy wondered who it was. I've told her you're the builder . . . the one who is coming to do the fence, yes. He's given me a quotation of a hundred and fifty pounds . . . yes, well, it's the nails . . . they're a hell of a price, nails. . . . No, they are not gold-plated ones. . . . What? . . . No, darling, it's Tuesday. You know you never come on a Tuesday evening. It's when Mummy and I go Old Time Dancing. . . . Well, it's her only pleasure these days. I can't possibly put it off. Now be a good boy and wait your turn. I mean when I'm not too busy with Mummy. . . . Tomorrow afternoon? . . . Well, I'd better see what her plans are, hold on. (*She covers the phone. Calling*) Darling?

Alec opens the bathroom door

Alec Yes?
Harriet What time are you coming tomorrow?
Alec Why?
Harriet Mummy wants me to go shopping in the afternoon.
Alec That's all right. As long as you're back by six.

Alec closes the bathroom door

Harriet (*returning to the phone*) Yes, darling, that's fine, as long as you're away by five-thirty . . . Bye. (*She replaces the receiver. She takes her diary and pen from the bedhead and jots it down*) "Eggs away five-thirty. Fish arrives at six." (*She closes the book and replaces it on the bedhead*)

Alec enters from the bathroom in shirt and trousers, carrying his jacket

Alec I've just weighed myself. I've put on four pounds.
Harriet Well it's not what you eat here, darling.
Alec Oh, no, it's not here, it's at home. Mildred's the best cook south of the Humber . . . her treacle parkin's out of this world. If I didn't come down here a couple of nights a week, I'd be out like a balloon.

Harriet (*getting out of bed and putting her housecoat on*) That reminds me, darling . . . The housekeeping. (*She turns the duvet back*)

She goes into the sitting-room followed by Alec

Alec What again?

Harriet It's a fortnight since you gave me the last lot.

Alec Oh, it can't be. I thought it was last week.

Harriet No, darling, that must have been Mildred's.

Alec I suppose it must have. We'll have to have a chat about this, Harriet. I mean there's hardly any difference between your housekeeping and Mildred's and she feeds three growing lads.

Harriet Well I do have Mummy.

Alec Well she must have an appetite like a bloody horse.

Harriet It's not like you, Alec . . . to be rude about my mother.

Alec I know, but she does go it a bit. I mean, she smokes like a chimney and gets through four bottles of vodka a week. Times are bad, Harriet. I've got six trawlers laid up at Grimsby, and that lot I've got in the Channel are doing me no good.

Harriet picks up the bills from the desk. He finishes dressing

Harriet There you are . . . I keep everything.

Alec Harriet, I trust you.

Harriet No, just look at the bills. I want you to look.

Alec All right then. (*He takes the bills to the desk, sits and examines them closely*)

Harriet Of course, we could put Mummy in a home if that's what you'd prefer.

Alec I don't hold anything against the woman. It's just that she's an extra mouth to feed . . . and times are bad. Look at this . . . not only vodka, Champagne.

Harriet It was Mummy's birthday. We had a few friends in.

Alec You must have had half of Brighton in. *Six bottles?*

Harriet We've two bottles left. Look I can't stand this bickering. I'll pay for it.

Alec No, it's not that, Harriet, but hasn't your mother any means of support apart from me?

Harriet Daddy left her penniless. It's all right though, I didn't want you to pay for it. I'll sell some jewellery my grandmother left me.

Alec Oh, don't start that. I'll pay the damn thing. It's just that for a woman with no money, she flings it about a bit. (*He gets his cheque book out*)

Harriet I'll speak to her.

Alec Just tell her times are hard. We've all got to tighten our belts. Nowadays, there are more fishermen than fish. It's like I've told Mildred, we've got to economize. I've got her mother to keep as well you know, apart from her three brothers and their families.

Harriet (*handing him a pen*) You mustn't let people take advantage of you.

Alec (*writing a cheque*) When I think of the number of people I'm support-ing . . . if anything happened to me, the whole social security system would collapse under the strain. (*He gives her a cheque*)

Harriet Thank you, darling, you're gorgeous.

She puts her arm around his neck and kisses him

Alec Don't start getting me going again. (*He gets up*)
Harriet All right we'll wait till this evening.
Alec Bye ... d'you really think there's any chance of us putting your mother into a home?
Harriet Well we could try, but it would be frightfully expensive. Shall I make some enquiries?
Alec (*going towards the front door*) Might not be a bad idea. But make damned sure it's a temperance one.

Alec exits

Black-out

SCENE 3

The same. Wednesday. Late afternoon

The Lights come up and Gordon is discovered doing up his tie in the bedroom. He walks into sitting-room, putting on his jacket

Gordon (*calling*) I'm just going to phone Magda.
Harriet (*off, in the kitchen*) Well hurry, it's after five-thirty.
Gordon (*starting to dial*) Do you want a drink, darling?
Harriet (*off*) No, Gordon, I'm making some tea.
Gordon Do you mind if I have one? (*Still holding the receiver he gets a glass, then a carafe of water, then a bottle of vodka from the shelf under the sofa table*)
Harriet (*off*) You've been drinking rather a lot lately.
Gordon (*holding up a nearly empty bottle*) It's your mother you ought to worry about, not me. She's had most of this. (*He pours the vodka into his glass, then pours a little water into the empty vodka bottle, swills it round and then empties the bottle into his glass ... shaking it to get the last drop. He then lifts the glass to his lips but puts it down on the table to speak into the phone*) Hello, Magda, it's me. The phone's been ringing for ages, where have you been? ... The hen house? ... Well, why isn't Freda laying? ... Oh all right, I'll have a word with her when I get back. ... Now don't start, Magda, I've had a very exhausting afternoon ... well you know what our clients are like. Nothing you can do pleases them ... a hell of an afternoon. ... No, Magda, I'm not trying to dodge your birthday party. I'll be there. I shall be leaving the office in a few minutes. I've just got a couple of letters to dictate and then I'm off. ... Yes, you go back to the hen house ... put a couple of golf balls under Freda. It might jog her memory. (*He replaces the receiver*)

Harriet, in a smart outfit, enters from the kitchen

Harriet Darling, I think the electric kettle's on the blink.

Gordon I don't want to know, I've just had Nagda magging me.
Harriet What?
Gordon Magda nagging me. I'll have to go.
Harriet I'm not asking you to look at it, I just wondered if we could afford an electrician.
Gordon Nobody can afford an electrician . . . see if your mother can fix it?
Harriet Mummy?
Gordon Well, you told me she mended the vacuum cleaner.
Harriet (*realizing*) Oh, yes, so she did. I'd forgotten.
Gordon (*giving her a kiss*) See you again on Friday.
Harriet Darling, I can hardly wait. I'll be counting the minutes.
Gordon Me too.

Harriet looks at her wristwatch and Gordon goes to the hall and picks up his briefcase. The doorbell rings. Harriet looks surprised

Harriet Hell . . .

Gordon, clutching his briefcase, comes rushing back to the sitting-room

Gordon Who can that be?
Harriet Must be Mummy. Go out of the back way through the kitchen.
Gordon Hang on, wouldn't this be a good time for me to meet her?
Harriet Certainly not. (*Pushing him towards the kitchen door*) Now off you go.

The doorbell rings again

Gordon exits through the kitchen door and slams it as he goes

(*She empties the ashtray, pours Gordon's vodka back into the bottle and then puts the glass, water carafe and bottle back on the table shelf. She composes herself, and then goes and opens the front door*) Anne!
Anne (*off*) Darling!
Harriet I don't believe it. Come in.

Anne enters. She is a smartly-dressed woman of about thirty with a bright personality. She is carrying a small suitcase

They come into the sitting-room

Anne I hope I haven't come at an awkward time.
Harriet (*taking the suitcase and putting it under the desk*) Course not. I just can't believe it's you. You look marvellous.
Anne *You* do, I feel a total wreck. I can't tell you how thrilled I am to see you.
Harriet I kept sending you Christmas cards but they came back address unknown. I'd given you up for dead.
Anne We moved to New Zealand.
Harriet Oh, well, I wasn't far wrong.
Anne I gave up writing to you when you and Bob went to South America.
Harriet I didn't stay there long. We split up.
Anne Oh, darling, I am sorry.
Harriet You needn't be, he turned out to be a crook.
Anne No. In what way?

Harriet In every way, fraud, embezzlement, robbery with violence, attempted murder.

Anne Not you I hope.

Harriet No, a very dear friend of ours. Awfully nice man, frightfully wealthy, and a judo expert. One day he was fooling around and put me in this rather complicated hold. Bob walked in, misunderstood, and threw him out the window.

Anne Was he hurt?

Harriet Deeply. Now tell me about Richard, is he still a vet?

Anne Yes. He administers to half the sheep on South Island.

Harriet Sounds very lucrative.

Anne It should be.

Harriet How on earth did you find me?

Anne Sheer chance. Someone gave me your mother's address in Sydney. So I rang her up and she told me where you were.

Harriet How long are you over for?

Anne I'm not sure.

Harriet Is Richard with you?

Anne No, he's not. We came over together, but we had another blinding row yesterday and I told him to clear off back home.

Harriet You mean without you?

Anne He couldn't care less. Nowadays he lives in an alcoholic haze. He tries to give it up occasionally, but he only needs one and bingo, he's flat on his back again.

Harriet So it's over?

Anne Finally and irrevocably.

Harriet Oh dear, where are you staying?

Anne I'll find a hotel.

Harriet Don't give it another thought, you're staying with me and the first thing you're going to have is a stiff drink ... I've got a drop of brandy somewhere. (*She gets a bottle and glass from the shelf of the sofa table*)

Anne This is a lovely flat, how long have you been here?

Harriet (*giving Anne the brandy*) About three years.

Anne Thanks.

Harriet Just after I met Alec.

Anne Oh, you've remarried?

Harriet Not exactly.

Anne Ah ...

Harriet He's a—a friend.

Anne Well that's the sort of friend to have, dear.

Harriet And then if you're here at the weekend, you'll meet another friend.

Anne Oh, lovely, who?

Harriet Gordon.

Anne And doesn't Alec mind?

Harriet He doesn't know.

Anne You mean they've never met?

Harriet And please God they never will.

Anne (*after a pause*) Do you ... er ... with Gordon?

Harriet Yes.

Anne And do you ... er ... with Alec?

Harriet Yes I "err" with both of them. But not at the same time.

Anne Darling, how exciting. A husband in Peru and two boyfriends, which one pays the rent?

Harriet They both do. It's the only way I can keep this place up.

Anne You must be rolling in it.

Harriet No, dear, they've both got wives to support. It doesn't leave much over for little luxuries like me.

Anne Don't you get a feeling of guilt when you think of their wives?

Harriet No, darling, I'm not trying to break up their marriages. I wouldn't dream of it.

Anne But they're both sleeping with you.

Harriet Well, yes, but just because a man hops in a taxi once in a while, doesn't mean he's got to get rid of his car. Anyway, I've already had a husband and I don't want any more thank you.

Anne How do you keep them apart?

Harriet I found it a bit tricky at first until I thought of Mummy. She's very pure and strait-laced.

Anne *Your mother?*

Harriet Not the mother you know. This is a mythical mother who'd die of shock if ever she knew I was a kept woman.

Anne And it works?

Harriet It has so far, thank heavens. My whole livelihood depends on it. If I lose one of them I'm out on my ear.

Anne Well I've lost mine.

Harriet Never mind.

Anne I wonder what went wrong with my Richard?

Harriet Darling, what goes wrong with any of them?

Anne I suppose it could have been me.

Harriet Absolute rubbish. I married a real charmer and look how he turned out. I certainly didn't make him turn to crime and women any more than you caused Richard to become an alcoholic. The tendencies were already built in. They're like electric toasters, once they go wrong you might as well chuck 'em out and get a new one.

Anne I suppose you're quite an authority on men by now.

Harriet There's nothing to be an authority about. They're incredibly basic, they have none of our finesse, and subtlety.

Anne Don't you ever get bored?

Harriet I haven't time, darling, I'm far too busy. I'm running a minor industry.

Anne And quite a successful one.

Harriet Yes, I'm working double shifts. (*She looks at her watch*) And the evening one starts any minute now.

Anne Are they both generous?

Harriet As generous as they can afford to be.

Anne Having two customers helps.

Harriet Anne, dear, don't be crude.

Anne You admit to having two.

Harriet The number is immaterial, it's the word customer I take exception to. I'm a mistress.

Anne Yes, but to two men.

Harriet Not as far as they are concerned. And if there wasn't an economic crisis right now I could manage very happily with one. I dare say if you're a vet with a practice of half a million sheep you're not short of a bob or two, but over here everyone is having to make sacrifices, and it's been a very bad year for kept women. Tea and cakes?

Anne Just some tea would be lovely.

Harriet I'll have to boil the water in a saucepan.

Anne Why?

Harriet The kettle's broken and I've still got some washing-up to do.

Harriet exits to the kitchen

Anne Don't your lovers ever help you?

Harriet (*off*) No. That'll be the day.

Alec enters from the front door with a plastic carrier bag

They've both been spoilt by indulgent wives.

Alec Who has?

Anne I beg your pardon?

Alec Who's been spoilt?

Harriet hurries back in

Harriet Hello, darling. (*She kisses him*) We've just been talking about husbands. Hers and mine. This is my friend Alec. Alec, this is Anne.

Alec How d'you do, Anne.

Anne How do you do.

Harriet I'm just making some tea, will you have a cup?

Alec All right. And then I've got to nip along to Newhaven.

Harriet What now?

Alec I'll only be an hour or so, one of the trawlers has run aground.

Harriet Is everybody all right?

Alec Oh, yes, they can all walk off. They've had enough practice. Oh—(*he hands her the plastic bag*)—I thought I'd drop this off. It's our supper.

Harriet (*brightly*) Oh, cod?

Alec It's best halibut.

Harriet That's a change.

Alec It'll make a change from all those bloody omelettes.

Harriet The eggs are a present from Mummy, she likes them.

Alec Likes them? I reckon she lays them.

Harriet You two make some small talk while I'm in the kitchen and do keep off controversial subjects.

Alec Such as what?

Harriet Morals, matrimony . . . and Mummy.

Harriet exits to the kitchen

Anne and Alec eye each other

Alec Just popped in have you?
Anne Yes.
Alec Live locally?
Anne New Zealand.
Alec Oh, New Zealand, eh? I was there when I was in the Navy.
Anne Really.
Alec I spent a few weeks in Windy Wellington with a bent shaft.
Anne Sounds painful.
Alec (*laughing*) Very. How long are you over for?
Anne Well, it's sort of indefinite.
Alec Where are you staying?
Anne Harriet very kindly said I could stay with her.
Alec Any friend of Harriet's is a friend of mine. You're very welcome.
Anne Thank you.
Alec Harriet's told you about us, I suppose.
Anne Yes, she has.
Alec She's a grand girl. Have you known her long?
Anne Yes, ever since we were kids, I always looked upon her as a sister.
Alec Oh. Then no doubt you know her mother.
Anne Yes, I do.
Alec Sanctimonious old trout. Got religion, you know.
Anne Oh really?
Alec She's probably a very nice woman underneath, but despite all that psalm singing and good works she can't half knock it back. (*He mimes drinking*) Did you know Harriet's husband?
Anne Only slightly.
Alec Mad Bob they call him. He's in and out the nick in Peru.
Anne So I've heard.
Alec But I gather Harriet's mother's still very loyal to his memory, thinks the sun shines out of his trousers. And what about your husband? What does he do?
Anne He's a vet.
Alec That's a worthy vocation. A man of loving kindness, eh?
Anne Yes, to animals but not to me. I think I'd be all right if I had four legs.
Alec He ought to team up with Harriet's mother, she's got hollow ones.

Harriet enters with a tray of tea

Harriet Despite what you may think I've never known her the worse for drink.
Alec No, it probably improves her.
Harriet (*pouring the tea*) Here we are, and go easy on the sugar, dear.
Alec Stop nagging, Harriet. It's my only weakness, apart from you that is. (*He blows her a kiss and helps himself to sugar*)
Harriet I keep telling him all that sugar can't be good for him.

Alec jerks his cup and spills some tea on his trousers

Alec Oh hell. (*He puts the cup down and feels for a hanky*) I haven't got a hanky.
Harriet Your clean ones are back from the laundry.

Alec Can you get me one?
Harriet You've got the key.
Alec Oh, yes. (*To Anne*) We have to keep my things locked away in case her mother sees them. I'm not supposed to be here.

Alec goes into the bedroom and shuts the door. He unlocks the top drawer and takes out a pocket hanky and relocks the drawer. Then he dabs at his clothes. During this Harriet and Anne continue speaking

Anne He's sweet, isn't he?
Harriet Yes. (*She looks at the tray*) Oh, sorry, I forgot the cake. Would you like some?
Anne Yes, please, I'm famished.
Harriet When did you last eat?
Anne I had a slice of toast at breakfast.
Harriet Oh, you silly thing, you should have said something. Come into the kitchen and I'll run you up a batch of omelettes.
Anne Oh, thanks.

Harriet and Anne exit into the kitchen. Gordon enters from the front door and looks around

Gordon Harriet?

Harriet appears at the kitchen doorway and is transfixed

Harriet Gordon.
Gordon Sorry, darling. Magda's birthday. I left her present in my drawer. (*He goes to the bedroom door*)

Alec exits to the bathroom

Harriet daren't shout out as Gordon walks into the bedroom. She stands at the kitchen door, closes her eyes and awaits the inevitable. Gordon goes to his drawer, unlocks it, rummages around, takes out a small jewel box and closes the drawer. He then opens the box to admire the ring, but it falls out and rolls under the bed

(*Muttering*) Oh, hell. (*He bends down beside the bed and starts groping for it, almost ending up under the bed*)

Alec comes out of the bathroom, zipping up his flies, and walks straight out of the bedroom into the sitting-room without seeing Gordon. He walks over to his tea and drinks it

Alec Lovely. (*He walks over and gives Harriet a kiss*) See you . . . I won't be long.

Alec exits through the front door

Harriet, still frozen with fright, tiptoes into the bedroom

Harriet Gordon.
Gordon (*getting up from beside the bed*) Found it, damned thing rolled right under.
Harriet You, er . . . you didn't notice anything?

Gordon Bit of fluff, that's all.
Harriet (*relieved*) Ah, well, the hoover's not working again.
Gordon You're a pair, you and Magda. You've only got to look at a household appliance and it stops. (*He crosses out of the bedroom into the sitting-room*)
Harriet (*following*) Look, darling, I do wish you wouldn't come without phoning first. Mummy could have been here.
Gordon You told me yesterday she wasn't coming till this evening.
Harriet Oh, did I?
Gordon Yes.
Harriet Ah, well that's true, she isn't.
Gordon Then what are you making a fuss about?

Anne enters and stops on seeing Gordon

Harriet Oh, this is my friend, Anne, from New Zealand.
Gordon How do you do.
Anne Hello.
Harriet Anne, this is Gordon.
Anne (*reacting nervously and shooting furtive glances around the room, looking for Alec*) Oh, how do you do, Gordon. We've just made some tea. Would you like some?
Gordon No thanks, I haven't time.
Harriet Oh, please, just for a few minutes.
Gordon No, I'm organizing Magda's party. We've got half of Reigate coming.
Harriet Just stop and say hello to Anne.
Anne I've heard so much about you.
Gordon (*warily*) Have you?
Harriet It's all right, darling, she knows about us.
Gordon In that case I'll have a quick beer.
Harriet You know where it is.
Gordon Yes, in the fridge. (*To Anne*) Nice to meet you.

Gordon exits into the kitchen

Anne You certainly know how to pick 'em dear. I've been wasting my time in New Zealand.

There is a loud crash and shout from the kitchen

Harriet God, what have you done?

Gordon crawls in

Gordon I've broken my leg.
Harriet How?
Gordon I slipped on a bloody fish!
Harriet Oh, my God.
Gordon Help me into bed.
Harriet There isn't time.
Gordon Isn't time for what?
Harriet Before you go home.

Anne You've got to leave at any moment.
Gordon I can't. I'm in agony. Help me on to the bed and get a doctor.

They help him through to the bedroom

Harriet But Magda's birthday party.
Gordon It's agony.
Anne No, you may enjoy it.
Gordon I mean my leg. Now steady, let me down gently.

They jerk him up on to the bed

Harriet You can't stay.
Gordon Just ring for the doctor.
Harriet No, they never come out for little things.
Gordon Little things? It's broken
Harriet Have a look at it Anne.
Anne (*removing his sock and shoe*) I think I ought to take his trousers off.
Harriet I think not, it's only his ankle that needs looking at.
Anne (*feeling his ankle and calf*) Lie back.
Gordon Ooo ... ah ... careful!
Anne Be quiet.
Gordon Are you sure she knows what she's doing?
Harriet Course she does. Her husband's a vet!
Anne I'll just make absolutely sure it's not broken. (*She pushes the ball of the foot back*)
Gordon *Ow!*
Anne Now what?
Gordon You've made it worse.
Anne Nonsense
Gordon You have.
Harriet She's done this to sheep all over New Zealand.
Gordon Then she ought to be investigated by the RSPCA.
Anne It's only a sprain.
Gordon Fat lot you know.
Anne Have you got a bandage?
Harriet In the bathroom cabinet.

Anne exits to the bathroom

You ought to be in hospital.
Gordon I don't want to go to hospital. I hate hospitals.
Harriet Then go home.
Gordon That's even worse. Magda can't bear anyone to be ill, it upsets her, especially on her birthday.
Harriet You can't possibly stay here.
Gordon Why not?
Harriet Because Mummy's coming round.
Gordon Let her. You can tell her I'm the paper hanger and fell off a ladder.
Harriet Don't be stupid.
Gordon I've been avoiding your mother for two years. I don't mind it when I'm in good health, but when I'm injured and suffering the most

excruciating pain I am not prepared to put myself out for the delicate susceptibilities of a gin-swilling pillar of the Anglican church.

Harriet I think that's an awfully cruel thing to say about my mother. She does not swill gin.

Gordon All right, vodka.

Anne enters with a roll of bandage

Harriet I hope if you ever meet her you'll apologize.

Anne The chances are he will.

Harriet I'd better ring her. (*She goes into the sitting-room, shutting the bedroom door behind her, goes to the phone and dials*)

Anne (*winding the bandage on his ankle*) I'm sure if you made an effort you could walk on it.

Gordon Walk on it!?

Anne Well, with a stick.

Gordon What's the point?

Anne So you can go home.

Harriet (*into the phone*) Hello, is that Newhaven Harbour? . . . I want to leave a message for Mr Bulthorpe . . . you haven't got a pen? Well hang on I'll see if I can find you one. . . . (*She starts to move away and reacts*) Well, see if you can find a pencil, its urgent.

Gordon I don't want to go home, not in this condition. I want to lie down, and if I go home I shall have to sit up and be jolly with all her brainless friends.

Anne She'll wonder what's happened to you?

Gordon I'll ring her to say I'm in hospital with a broken leg. She'll be furious of course.

Anne She might want to come and see you.

Gordon Only to break the other one.

Anne (*finishing bandaging*) Is that better?

Gordon Not much. Would you mind just plumping up the pillows behind me?

Anne does so

And straightening the bed?

She walks round the bed, flicking the cover disdainfully, ending by giving the duvet a sharp yank, which hurts his leg

Ow!

Anne Is that all?

Gordon No, I'd like a drink.

Anne goes into the sitting-room, slamming the bedroom door behind her

Anne He's not very good in bed, is he?

Harriet What do you mean?

Anne He never stops complaining.

Harriet (*into the phone*) Oh, good you found some chalk . . . well the message is, tell Mr Bulthorpe that Mummy's had one of her nasty turns and I've had to put her to bed. . . . Goodbye. (*She replaces the receiver*)

Anne (*pouring a vodka*) What do we do about Gordon?
Harriet (*dialling again*) We'll get a cab, shove him in it and send him home.
Anne He doesn't want to go home.
Harriet Then he can drive round Brighton all night. Oh, damn, it's engaged, it's always engaged. It's easier to go into the street and stop one. Hold the fort, I'll be right back.

Harriet dashes out through the front door

Anne takes the drink into Gordon

Anne Here you are.
Gordon What is it?
Anne Vodka.
Gordon Oh, thanks.
Anne Will that be all, sir?
Gordon I think so. Where's Harriet?
Anne Just popped out, but I am at your service.
Gordon Are you? Then get me some ice for this. (*He holds out his glass*)
Anne (*taking it*) Oh, sir, your wishes are my command. (*She goes to the door*)
Gordon And while you're at it, some lemon.
Anne (*turning in the doorway*) What did the last servant die of? (*She goes into the sitting-room and towards the kitchen*)
Gordon (*calling*) I say!
Anne Yes?
Gordon D'you know what I really fancy?
Anne (*stopping*) Tell me before I swoon with ecstacy.
Gordon A nice boiled egg.
Anne Oh, you kinky devil. Three minute?
Gordon No, I can't eat an egg under four minutes.
Anne Well try, and I'll time you.

Anne exits into the kitchen

Gordon dials a number on the phone. He winces and rearranges his position

Gordon Hello, Magda, it's me . . . look I've had the most awful accident . . . no not in the car. I stepped on a fish and I've broken a leg or something. . . . What do you mean paddling? No of course I wasn't paddling, the fish was on the floor . . . the floor of the fish shop. . . . Yes I was getting you some smoked salmon for your birthday and I trod on this damned fish . . . how do I know? A halibut I think. . . . Am I going to sue? No of course I'm not going to sue. How can you sue a halibut? . . . Magda stop asking me stupid questions. The point is I can't get back for your party. . . . Well, I'm in bed, I can't move . . . . It's a nursing home. . . . I've no idea, I didn't see the name, they just brought me in on a stretcher. . . . Well there's nobody to ask . . . all right I'll try. (*Calling*) Nurse! Nurse!

Anne pokes her head out of the kitchen

Anne Oh, belt up!

Anne returns to the kitchen

Gordon Did you hear that, Magda? . . . Yes, that's what they're like in here
. . . dreadful place, but it's only for tonight. I'll hobble back to you in the
morning. You'll just have to cope without me. . . . Yes, all right, I'll give
you the number—it's o-two-seven-three, five-five-o-two-one . . . yes,
darling, I'll try and get a bit of sleep and you shall have your present in the
morning. . . . Happy birthday . . . bye, bye. (*He replaces the receiver*)

*Anne enters from the kitchen with Gordon's glass containing ice and lemon
and goes to the bedroom*

Anne There you are, ice and lemon.
Gordon You're very kind. How's my egg doing?
Anne About two minutes to lift-off.
Gordon And could I have some very thin brown bread and lots of butter?
Anne You sensuous beast. Would you like me to fan you while you eat it?
Gordon How very kind.
Anne I'll go and put my yashmak on.

Gordon laughs

Alec enters through the front door and comes into the sitting-room

Anne comes into the sitting-room, slamming the bedroom door behind her

Alec What's up?
Anne Oh, Alec.
Alec Who's in the bedroom?
Anne The bedroom?
Alec Yes, the bedroom, who's in there? Doesn't sound like Harriet.
Anne No, she's gone to post a letter. I thought you'd gone to Newhaven.
Alec No, I phoned through and checked. It wasn't my boat. Now who's in
that bedroom?
Anne My husband.
Alec Your husband?
Anne Yes.
Alec I thought he was in New Zealand.
Anne Yes, he was, but he's here now.
Alec Oh, that's nice for you, but what's he doing in my bedroom?
Anne Well, he had an accident. He stepped on a fish.
Alec Stepped on it? What was he doing, paddling?
Anne No, no, it was in the kitchen.
Alec Oh, dear.
Anne He's broken his leg and he can't be moved.
Alec That's awkward.
Anne Very.
Alec Would you care for a drink?
Anne Oh, thank you.
Alec What'll you have?
Anne A glass of sherry, please.
Alec Good idea. I'll join you. (*He gets the drinks*) How about your husband,
what's his name by the way?
Anne Gordon. (*Quickly*) Richard.

Alec Gordon Richards?

Anne No Richard, that's his name but some people call him Gordon, that's his other name.

Alec Will he have a drink?

Anne Not for the moment, in fact not at all.

Alec Eh?

Anne He doesn't drink, or smoke or anything like that. He's a bit religious.

Alec Oh, another one of those.

Anne In fact he's a lay preacher and that's what worries me.

Alec What does?

Anne You and Harriet.

Alec Oh you mean the fact that we're er . . .

Anne Exactly. He's terribly old fashioned about these sort of things, and so we've had to tell him that you and Harriet are man and wife. I hope you don't mind.

Alec No, I don't mind, only Harriet's already got a husband in Peru.

Anne Yes I know, so that's who you'll have to be. Mad Bob.

Alec Mad Bob?

Anne Yes, Harriet's husband Bob from Peru.

Alec I see.

Anne If he should ask you anything about Peru . . .

Alec I've never been to Peru.

Anne Neither's he.

Alec Are you sure?

Anne Pretty sure.

Alec Damn it, you must know, you're married to him.

Anne Yes, but there's a whole chapter of his life that he doesn't talk about.

Alec Really. Here's your sherry.

Anne Thank you. You see, before I met him, he'd had some awful experiences he won't talk about, and it may well have been in Peru.

Alec Oh. What do you think it was that happened to him?

Anne I've no idea, but sometimes at night, he screams out things in his sleep.

Alec Like what?

Anne "Help", or "let go of it".

Alec What could they have got hold of in Peru?

Anne I'm not sure it was Peru, I'm more inclined to think it was New Guinea, because I know he spent a long time there.

Alec New Guinea. Oh, well there's no knowing what could've got hold of him out there.

Anne And he's developed a sort of mental block.

Alec Oh, poor chap.

Anne So you'll make allowances.

Alec Naturally.

Anne If he starts rambling a little, it was those lost years.

Harriet enters hurriedly from the front door

Harriet There's not a cab in the whole of—— (*Seeing Alec*) Alec!

Alec Cab, I thought you went out to post your letter.

Harriet (*blankly*) What?

Anne Yes, it was for me, she was trying to catch the last post at the main office.

Harriet Yes.

Anne It was to Richard's mother saying that he had arrived here safely. (*She points to the bedroom*)

Harriet Oh, yes. Very safely.

Alec Safely? What do you mean safely? He's broken his leg.

Harriet Yes. Apart, of course, from his broken leg.

Anne Richard is having a sleep now.

Harriet Oh, good. Tell me has Alec met your husband yet?

Alec No, not yet. You see Anne had to explain the problem to me.

Harriet Oh good, I'm so glad. Which particular problem was that?

Alec The one about us not being married.

Harriet Ah, that one.

Alec She told me how upset her husband'd be, if he knew we weren't married, only living together.

Harriet I see.

Alec She told him I'm your husband Bob from Peru.

Harriet She's what?

Anne No, I haven't told him yet, dear, I thought I'd leave that one for you.

Harriet Oh, thank you. What a good idea, how clever of you.

Alec We're just having a drink, love. What would you like?

Harriet I would like a very stiff vodka.

Alec Right. (*He goes to pick up the bottle*) This damned bottle's empty.

Harriet Oh, is it?

Alec It's your mother again.

Harriet (*to Anne*) Mummy's staying with my sister at Folkestone. She's not well.

Alec I'm not surprised the way she knocks it back. What'll you have instead?

Harriet I would've liked a vodka.

Alec Do you want me to go out and get a bottle?

Harriet Oh please, would you, darling?

Alec (*going to the hall*) Anything else you want?

Harriet I don't think so.

Alec Right.

He exits

Harriet When did he come?

Anne Soon after you left?

Harriet I'd better nip and tell Gordon. (*She goes towards the bedroom*)

Anne Tell him his egg's on the way.

Harriet His what?

Anne Never mind.

Anne exits to the kitchen

Harriet (*going into the bedroom*) Gordon.

Gordon (*feebly*) Oh hello, Harriet, where've you been?

Harriet (*switching on the bedside light*) I went to see about Mummy. Darling, I've got some rather bad news.

Gordon I don't want to hear it.
Harriet Well you'd better. Are you sitting comfortably?
Gordon No, what a stupid thing to say. I've got a broken leg and every muscle's torn to shreds, and I can't move an inch.
Harriet My husband's turned up.
Gordon What! (*He leaps out of bed and screams as his bad foot hits the floor*)
Harriet Careful!
Gordon Mad Bob? He'll kill me.
Harriet No he won't.
Gordon You said yourself how violent he is, he's a gangster.
Harriet Just get back into bed.
Gordon That's why you left him, because he was so jealous.
Harriet No.
Gordon Remember what you said he did to that man in Peru?
Harriet That was years ago.
Gordon If he could do that to a Judo expert in peak condition, what's he going to do to a man with a broken leg?
Harriet He doesn't know you.
Gordon That won't stop him.
Harriet Get back into bed and listen. You don't have to worry about Bob. We've told him you're Anne's husband.
Gordon (*getting into bed*) What?
Harriet As far as he's concerned, you've flown in from New Zealand, fell over a fish and broken your leg.
Gordon Who'd believe that?
Harriet He would.
Gordon He's not very bright is he?
Harriet Not frightfully.
Gordon All brawn and nothing up top.
Harriet That's why I left him for you. I had to have a man who was intelligent and sensitive, like you.
Gordon Yes, I suppose that's understandable. (*He groans*) I wish my leg wasn't so damn sensitive. I bet you could snap his off and he wouldn't even notice.
Harriet Anyway, darling, the point is you're supposed to have lived in New Zealand, you're a vet and you're married to Anne, and your name is Richard.
Gordon I see.
Harriet Can you remember that?
Gordon I suppose so, but does he have to come in here?
Harriet Only to go to the bathroom.
Gordon I'll just lie here and groan in agony.
Harriet That's right, darling, just play for sympathy. Now is there anything else I can get for you?
Gordon I wouldn't mind another vodka.
Harriet You'll have to wait, Bob's gone out to get some more. (*She sits cosily beside him and puts her arm around him*)
Gordon Careful.
Harriet I'm not near your leg.

Gordon No, I mean supposing he comes back and catches us.
Harriet He won't, relax.
Gordon How long is he over for?
Harriet Only a day or so.
Gordon What's he come for?
Harriet A conference, I think.
Gordon You told me he was a fugitive from justice.
Harriet Sort of.
Gordon Good God, do they have conferences now?

Anne enters from the kitchen with a tray containing a boiled egg etc. and goes to the bedroom during following dialogue

Harriet Would you like the television in here? You could watch the news.
Gordon No, I'm ill enough as it is without that.

Anne enters the bedroom

Anne What are you doing on the bed with my husband?
Gordon Oh, don't you start.
Harriet That's no way to speak to your wife.
Anne Anybody fancy a hard-boiled egg?
Gordon No, take it away.

She puts it on the chest of drawers

And I would appreciate a little peace.
Harriet You've got two little pieces now. Don't be greedy.
Gordon Just go and get me that vodka.
Harriet All right, darling.

Anne and Harriet go into the sitting-room and shut the bedroom door

Anne It may be a little premature, but have you considered where we're all going to sleep?
Harriet Oh God, no. There's only a single bed in the spare room.
Anne If you like I could stay at a hotel.
Harriet Oh no you don't. I need you here. Alec would think it a bit odd if you cleared off and left a sick husband. Alec and I will just have to make do with the spare room.
Anne Can you manage on a single bed?
Harriet He can manage it anywhere. There's nothing else for it, you'll just have to sleep in here on a sofa.
Anne Won't Alec think that rather odd?
Harriet Why?
Anne Well, we're supposed to be married.
Harriet I see, and what exactly have you in mind? Hopping into bed and sleeping with Gordon?
Anne Good heavens no, not technically sleeping, sort of bundling.
Harriet Sounds even worse.
Anne You've heard of bundling, haven't you?
Harriet No.
Anne Courting couples used to do it in the old days. You went to bed fully

dressed with a bolster between you. It was their equivalent of the pill.
Harriet What was?
Anne The bolster.
Harriet I bet that took a bit of swallowing.

Alec enters with bottle of vodka

Alec Here we are. Refreshments. (*He starts to pour vodka and tonics*)
Harriet While you're at it, pour one for Gor——Richard will you?
Alec Anne told me he was teetotal.
Harriet Did she? Well I wish somebody had told me.
Alec You've got to be careful how you behave with him around, he's very
  puritanical.
Harriet Oh, is he? Then I shall have to handle him with kid gloves.
Anne Yes I'm sure he'd enjoy that.
Alec Here's your drink, Harriet.
Harriet Thank you. By the way, darling, we're sleeping in the spare room
  tonight.
Alec Why?
Harriet Because Gordon—Richard is in our bed.
Alec Well Gordon Richard can go in the spare room.
Harriet There's only a single bed in there and he's got a bad leg.
Alec He's only got to lie on it, not ride it. Are we having anything to eat this
  evening?
Harriet Yes all right, what would you like?
Anne Nice hard-boiled egg?
Alec To hell with your hard-boiled eggs, let's have the halibut.
Harriet I suppose it's still edible.
Alec What do you mean?
Harriet That's the one that Richard flattened.
Anne I'll see if I can knock it into shape again.

Anne exits into the kitchen

Alec Now what are we doing about him, I want to sleep in my own bed.
Harriet I honestly don't think we ought to move him.
Alec Of course we can. I broke my leg on a trawler once and they hoisted me
  out with a winch.
Harriet I don't think we've got a winch.
Alec I'll go and have a word with him.
Harriet No. We'll handle it later. Have your drink whilst Anne and I go and
  see what we can do with that fish.
Alec Could we have it fried?
Harriet Why not? It's already been battered.

Harriet exits into the kitchen

Alec goes into the bedroom, carrying his glass

Alec Hey, you!

Gordon sits up nervously

Gordon Oh, you're Bob.
Alec That's right, from Peru. And you're Gordon Richard I take it.
Gordon No, no, just Richard.
Alec Oh, don't like being Gordon, eh?
Gordon Not very much.
Alec Brings back memories, eh?
Gordon What?
Alec Memories, you know New Guinea.
Gordon New Guinea?
Alec Don't remember a lot about that do you?
Gordon No, I don't think I do.
Alec Perhaps it's for the best, the brain blanks these things out.
Gordon It has in my case.
Alec You don't know what it was that got hold of you then?
Gordon No.
Alec Or even what it got hold of?
Gordon No, it's all a blank.
Alec You ought to be in hospital with that leg.
Gordon Oh, no, I hate hospitals.
Alec I suppose you had a basinful in Peru.
Gordon Peru?
Alec Your wife said you may have been there.
Gordon Did she? Well, I don't suppose I know it half as well as you do.
Alec No, I don't suppose you do.
Gordon In fact I think I was mostly over the border.
Alec What of?
Gordon Er—Equador!
Alec Nice place, Equador.
Gordon Very nice.
Alec Whereabouts in Equador were you?
Gordon Er ... (*Brightly*) In the capital.
Alec In the capital, yes ... what's it called?
Gordon Oh, yes, good heavens what's it called ...? How stupid ... it's on the tip of my tongue.
Alec Biggish place.
Gordon Oh biggish ... but not enormous.
Alec No, not enormous ... but biggish for Equador.
Gordon Oh, yes.
Alec Yes, you've just come from New Zealand, they tell me.
Gordon Yes, that's right.
Alec I was out there too.
Gordon (*with dismay*) Oh God! Were you?
Alec Twenty years ago.
Gordon Well you wouldn't recognize it now. It's all been changed.
Alec How about Wellington?
Gordon Oh that really has been changed.
Alec Do you know Christchurch?
Gordon Never been in it, but we could see the spire from our bedroom window.

Alec (*blankly*) Oh? Did you ever get to Hobart?
Gordon No, but I hear it's one of the prettiest parts of New Zealand.
Alec It's in Tasmania.
Gordon Is it? Well it's all been changed. (*Suddenly*) I've got it.
Alec What?
Gordon Quito. It's the capital.
Alec Not of Tasmania.
Gordon No, Equador.
Alec Oh yes.
Gordon Dear old Quito ... I wonder what it's like nowadays.
Alec You wouldn't recognize it.
Alec
Gordon } (*together*) It's all been changed.

Harriet enters from the kitchen and sees Alec is not there

Harriet Darling? Darling?
Alec In here, love.
Harriet Oh ... (*She dashes into the bedroom*) Well, what er—what exactly
  have you boys been talking about?
Alec Nothing much. Peru mostly.
Gordon And Equador.
Harriet I don't think you should brood on the past.
Alec Of course I know New Zealand better than Peru.
Gordon Oh.
Harriet Well it's awfully boring for me, I've never been there.
Alec I just thought there might be something we both had in common.
Harriet No, I wouldn't think so, dear.
Alec Well we've both covered the same territory you know.
Harriet Yes, I suppose you have.
Alec Of course, I was there long before he was.
Gordon I suppose you were, yes ... (*He points to Alec's drink*) Is that for me
  by the way?
Alec Oh no, I'm sorry I brought it in, tactless of me. I forgot you were
  teetotal. (*He drinks*)
Gordon So did I.
Alec Oh you haven't always been then?
Gordon Er ...
Harriet (*hastily*) I daresay it's all to do with his blank period.
Alec In New Guinea.
Harriet More than likely.
Alec You see if we could dig into your subconscious and look at whatever's
  been bothering you, you'd stop having those nightmares.
Gordon Oh those, yes, well I've got used to those.
Alec Your wife told me the horrors you go through.
Gordon My wife!
Harriet Anne.
Gordon Oh, that wife—er—my wife, Anne.
Harriet Yes, she's told us of the screaming, the gnashing of teeth. In fact she

wondered if it wouldn't be best for her to sleep out there on the sofa. (*To Gordon*) You don't mind, do you?

Gordon Anything you say, Harriet.

Alec In that case if you're sleeping in the spare room Harriet and I can have this bed.

Gordon Oh no, not with this leg. I prefer this bed. I'm used to it.

Alec How d'you mean, "*used to it*"?

Harriet He means this type of bed. I expect he's got one like this in New Zealand.

Gordon Yes, I expect I have.

Harriet Of course you have, you fool.

Gordon (*to Alec*) Of course I have, you fool!

Anne comes in from the kitchen, wearing an apron

Anne Harriet?

Harriet We're in here.

Anne goes to the bedroom

Anne I've burnt the halibut.

Alec How?

Anne I was frying and the fat caught fire.

Alec That settles it, we'll go out for dinner.

Harriet All four of us?

Alec Well not him, he's got a broken leg. Just you and me. Come on, Harriet, we'll have oysters, champagne, lobster and then a nice early night.

He takes the reluctant Harriet out of the bedroom and into the sitting-room

Harriet No wait—I've got to change.

Alec Well don't be long, I'll go and bring the car round.

Alec exits through the front door

Anne (*in the bedroom doorway*) You go and enjoy yourself. Don't worry about a thing and leave everything in my hands.

Anne exits to the kitchen

Harriet does a double-take and stamps her foot in frustration

Harriet I don't want to leave everything in her hands!

CURTAIN

ACT II

The same. Later that night

As the CURTAIN *rises Gordon is at the door of the bedroom in his pyjama jacket and dressing-gown.* He is hobbling with great pain and difficulty towards the sofa

He reaches it and sits as the front door slams and Anne appears with a bag containing two hamburgers

Anne What are you doing out of bed?
Gordon I got cramp in my leg.
Anne Oh dear . . . (*She puts down the bag*) Can I help?
Gordon No, no, it'll be all right, in fact it's gone. (*Giving a cry of pain*) Ow.
Anne Come back, has it?
Gordon No, that's the other leg, the one that's broken.
Anne (*patting him*) Oh we are in a state, aren't we?
Gordon Yes.
Anne I really think we should be in bed.
Gordon (*alarmed*) We?
Anne When comforting the sick we always use the first person plural.
Gordon How very singular of you.

Anne opens the bag

What have you got there?
Anne Hamburgers.
Gordon Couldn't you find the Chinese takeaway?
Anne (*sitting next to him*) No, it's been taken away altogether. It's a hamburger joint now.
Gordon I don't feel like a hamburger.
Anne There's not a lot else is there? I ate mine on the way home.

Gordon opens the container and lifts out the hamburger

Gordon I wish you'd eaten mine. (*He opens the hamburger and looks at the meat*) Ugh, it looks like a long-playing rissole.
Anne Come on, get stuck into it, you've got to keep your strength up. You'll need it later.
Gordon What for?
Anne Who knows, you might have to fight a duel to the death with Mad Bob.
Gordon I think it's a bit much Harriet gallivanting about with him, stuffing themselves stupid with lobster while I'm lying here with a bloody hamburger wondering how I'm going to pay the rent.
Anne She's got divided loyalties. It's very awkward for a woman in her position.

Gordon It's not too good for a man in mine. As soon as they come back they'll be going to bed together.

Anne Don't think about it, it'll only make your leg throb. Maybe nothing'll happen.

Gordon He's been on about his conjugal rights all evening.

Anne Perhaps she'll put a bolster between them.

Gordon That won't stop him, he's been up and down the Andes for years.

Anne Are you jealous?

Gordon Course I'm jealous.

Anne Let's look at the situation logically. Now that Harriet's husband is back, you've got to reorientate yourself and find another hobby.

Gordon What about you?

Anne What? As a hobby?

Gordon No, your domestic problem.

Anne Well, like you I married in haste and I'm going through a leisurely repentance.

Gordon Did you ever think about divorce?

Anne As I walked back down the aisle.

Gordon Yes, it wouldn't happen nowadays, they don't bother getting married. It's "hullo, darling, I fancy you", and they're into bed and on the list for a council house. No wonder half of 'em never get their 'O' levels.

Anne Anyway, I've finally seen the light and left him.

Gordon What didn't you like about him?

Anne You mean apart from the drinking, and the drinking?

Gordon Yes.

Anne Took me to New Zealand.

Gordon I wish to God somebody would take Magda. There's not a shred of pity in her. D'you know when I rang her up and told her I'd broken my leg, she——

Anne (*cutting in*) When you what?

Gordon Phoned to say I wouldn't be home.

Anne And told her you were here with Harriet?

Gordon Good God, no. I said I was in a private nursing home.

Anne Taking a bit of a risk, weren't you?

Gordon I had to tell her something, it's her birthday. Anyway she doesn't know the address I only gave her the phone number. I don't know why because she couldn't care less.

Anne That's the way Richard feels about me. He really wanted Harriet.

Gordon What? My Harriet?

Anne He only married me on the rebound.

Gordon That's why Magda married me.

Anne Odd, isn't it?

Gordon We're nothing but a pair of consolation prizes.

Anne Then let's console ourselves with a drink.

Gordon Good idea.

He gets up, hops a few paces and then shouts "Cramp!" and falls on Anne on the sofa

Alec and Harriet enter from the front door

Harriet I'll just see how the invalid . . . (*She sees them on the sofa*) What the hell is going on?
Gordon I'm stuck.
Harriet Darling.
Alec Yes.
Harriet I think you better get a crowbar.
Anne He got cramp and his leg's given away.
Harriet I hope that's all that's been given away.
Gordon I've seized up.
Harriet Have you?
Gordon And I can't move!
Harriet Darling, could you lift him off and get him back to bed.
Alec Come on, lad, up you get. (*He taps his bad leg*)
Gordon (*leaping up*) Ow!
Alec This way.

Alec takes Gordon's weight

Gordon Hang on, where are you taking me?
Alec To where you're going to sleep, in the spare room.
Gordon No.
Alec Harriet and I want that double bed.
Gordon Well, you can't have it!
Alec Are you going to try and stop me?
Gordon Good Lord no, it's just that I have to go in there first.
Alec Where?
Gordon In there to the bathroom. So if you could just help me.
Alec Shouldn't your wife be helping you?
Harriet ⎫
Anne   ⎬ (*together*) No!
Gordon ⎭
Harriet She's not strong enough. Off you go.

Alec and Gordon go into the bedroom. Harriet shuts the door and rounds on Anne

   During the following Alec and Gordon exit to the bathroom

Now then.
Anne Have a nice dinner?
Harriet Never mind that. What about you two?
Anne We had hamburgers.
Harriet Why is he up and about?
Anne Now, Harriet, surely you don't think I'm trying to take him off you?
Harriet Looks very like it. You were both on the sofa.
Anne He slipped and fell.
Harriet And you very nobly slipped underneath him to break his fall.
Anne Exactly.
Harriet Well from now on just let him free-fall.
Anne Oh come on, Harriet, let's face the truth. The jig's up.
Harriet What jig?

Anne You can't go back to the way you were with both of them. Gordon won't want to share you with Bob.

Harriet Bob's only here on a flying visit. First thing tomorrow he goes back to Peru and we'll go back to status quo.

Anne I don't think it'll work.

Harriet I'd be awfully grateful if you'd mind your own business and stop interfering with my domestic arrangements.

Anne All right. I won't do another thing, dear. I'll just go to bed. Goodnight. (*She goes towards the bedroom*)

Harriet Oh no you won't. You're sleeping on this sofa.

Anne As you wish. I'll just get undressed. (*She starts to undress, removing her dress and disclosing her underwear*)

Alec enters from the bathroom and goes into the sitting-room

Harriet Surely you can sleep in your dress?

Anne I don't want it all creased.

Alec (*eyeing Anne*) Don't mind me, lass, I'm a married man.

Harriet Alec, go to bed at once.

Alec Can't I have a drink?

Harriet I'll bring you one in.

Alec (*still looking at Anne*) Don't bother, I'll have it in here.

Harriet Get yourself into bed. You wanted an early night.

Alec Yes, but in the double bed.

Harriet No, darling, the single one.

Alec Going to be a bit cramped, aren't we?

Harriet It'll be like the single bed we had that night in Bermuda. Remember?

Alec Bermuda? (*Enthusiastically*) Not half! I'll get my pyjamas. (*He goes hurriedly into the bedroom, unlocks his drawer, and gets his pyjamas and dressing-gown out, locking the drawer after him*)

Anne What happened in Bermuda?

Harriet Mind your own business.

Anne I just wondered.

Harriet Are you going to prance around all night in your knickers?

Anne If there was a little more privacy I could take them off.

Harriet It's funny how little we know about our friends, isn't it?

Anne Why, what have you heard about them, do tell me?

Harriet I'm talking about you. I've just discovered what you are, a thoroughly immoral unscrupulous trollop.

Anne Hark who's talking.

Alec comes back into the sitting-room

Alec Harriet, love?

Harriet What?

Alec (*to Anne*) Forgive me interrupting, won't you?

Anne Certainly.

Harriet Into that bedroom!

She picks up Anne's dress, throws it over her head and pushes Anne through, shutting the bedroom door

Alec Spoil sport.
Harriet Now what d'you want?
Alec There are no sheets on the bed.
Harriet I'll get them.

Alec points to the bedroom

Alec (*hopefully*) Not in there are they?
Harriet No they're not.

She pushes Alec out and they exit through the hall L

Gordon enters the bedroom from the bathroom

Gordon By jove! I feel better already.
Anne I'm so sorry, I'll cover up. (*She picks up her suitcase*)
Gordon (*getting into bed*) No, it's all right, doesn't bother me, I'm married.
Anne I've just had a severe reprimand from Harriet. (*She gets her négligé from the suitcase, puts it on, and puts her dress in the suitcase*)
Gordon Why?
Anne She feels we are getting too friendly.
Gordon I couldn't care less. She's making no attempt to get rid of that ghastly husband of hers. It's quite obvious that she's still attracted to him.
Anne Some women like violent men. (*She puts the suitcase on the wicker chair*)
Gordon Yes. And you can see what sort of lout he is. He ought to be on television doing beer commercials.
Anne Personally I prefer suave, sophisticated and intelligent men.
Gordon Well we're a dying breed you know. His lot's going to inherit the earth.
Anne Yes, I'm afraid so.

Harriet enters from the hall L *and goes towards the bedroom door*

Gordon It's all such a mess. I've already got a problem with Magda, and now I've got another one with Harriet.
Anne Don't worry, it'll all come out in the wash.
Gordon It'll need a pretty strong detergent.

They laugh. She sits on the bed. Harriet bursts into the bedroom

Harriet Oh, very cosy.
Anne Don't you knock when you come into a bedroom?
Harriet Not when it's mine. You ought to be ashamed of yourselves, it's disgraceful.
Gordon Harriet, we're only talking.
Harriet (*to Anne*) Just what are you doing?
Anne I was on my way to the bathroom and stopped for a chat.
Harriet If I were you, darling, I'd continue on your journey and have a nice long bath.
Anne Anything you say, darling. (*She gets up and goes towards the bathroom*) Won't be long.

She goes in with a cheeky smile

Harriet Have a cold shower too. (*She pulls the door shut*) Oh, darling, if you knew how much I've been missing you, if only you knew the agony I've been through.
Gordon That swine. What's he done?
Harriet Nothing. It's the mental agony of being so near to you and yet so helpless. It's been sheer torture for me, yearning to feel your arms around me.
Gordon What about that hooligan husband of yours?
Harriet Forget him.
Gordon Come off it, Harriet, he's been drooling about it all evening.
Harriet Nonsense.
Gordon That's what he's come back for.
Harriet No, there's been nothing like that between us for years. (*She sits on the bed next to Gordon*) You're the only man in my life.

The doorbell rings

Damn!
Gordon What's that?
Harriet Nothing.
Gordon It's the doorbell.
Harriet Ignore it.
Gordon It means there's somebody there.
Harriet Oh all right. (*She gets up hastily and goes into the sitting-room, shutting the door*)

The doorbell rings again

Oh God. How I wish it could be Mother. (*She goes to the hall*)

Gordon gets back under the covers as the following voices are heard in the hall. Harriet opens the front door

Richard (*off*) Hullo, Harriet.
Harriet Richard!
Richard (*off*) Forgive me, I know it's late.
Harriet You can't come in.
Richard (*off*) I must.

Richard enters. He is in his late thirties and looks slightly dishevelled. He carries a bottle of whisky wrapped in tissue paper

He goes into the sitting-room followed by Harriet

Harriet I'm just going to bed.
Richard I'm sorry but I'm feeling pretty ghastly.
Harriet Have you been drinking?
Richard No, why should you think that?
Harriet No reason. I just thought it's rather late to call on someone out of the blue.
Richard As a matter of fact I haven't had a drink for twenty-four hours.
Harriet Oh? So what's that in your hand?
Richard A present for you. Chocolates.

Harriet Thank you (*She removes the wrapper*) It's whisky.
Richard Is it? I thought they'd made a mistake. You remember Anne?
Harriet Of course I remember her. (*She puts the bottle on the table*)
Richard Well we've parted, bust up, caput.
Harriet Oh dear. You and Anne?
Richard She's cleared off and left me.
Harriet (*keeping an eye on the bedroom door*) Oh dear, well let's have lunch tomorrow and you can tell me all about it.
Richard No, it's now or never.
Harriet No, Richard. After all she's my oldest friend and considering the life you've led her——
Richard (*cutting in*) Life I've led her? How d'you know what sort of life I've led her?
Harriet You must have led her some sort of life or she would never have left you.
Richard What about the life she's led me?
Harriet Can't it keep till tomorrow? You've really called at the most awkward time, I'm trying to get to bed.
Richard Yes, yes, of course, I'm sorry. I'll go. (*He sits down*) How's Bob?
Harriet I've no idea.
Richard God, have you split up as well? (*He gets up*)
Harriet Yes, and I'll give you all the sordid details tomorrow.
Richard Oh, Harriet, this is marvellous.
Harriet What?
Richard You're free, I'm free, we're all free.
Harriet Not Bob, he's doing time in Peru.
Richard Look, I've been carrying a torch for you for years.
Harriet Well blow it out, dear.
Richard But I love you, Harriet. I've always loved you. I've come thirteen thousand miles for one of your smiles.
Harriet (*raising her eyes to heaven*) Oh Mammy.
Richard Mammy? Is she here?
Harriet Yes she is. And that's why you'd better go.
Richard I thought she was in Sydney.
Harriet She's just popped over for a few days.
Richard I'll be very quiet. But don't you see, Harriet, now that Bob's gone and Anne's gone, there's nothing to stop us coming together.
Harriet I'm afraid there is.
Richard You mean you've found somebody else?
Harriet Yes.
Richard Oh, God this is awful. (*He collapses into a chair and cups his head in his hands*) Awful.
Harriet Not for me.
Richard If only you'd told me.
Harriet Why should I have to keep you informed?
Richard No, I suppose I've got no claim on you except that of undying love. Give me a drink.
Harriet No, Richard.
Richard (*loudly*) Give me a drink!

Harriet Sh! Yes, all right, but I've only got brandy.
Richard I only want brandy.

She pours it

Where is he?
Harriet Where's who?
Richard This man you've taken up with. I want to see him.
Harriet Why?
Richard I want to congratulate him on his good fortune winning you. (*He takes the drink and the bottle from Harriet. He drains the brandy in one gulp*)
Harriet You've had your drink, now go, while you still can.
Richard I want to meet him and tell him he's taken the only girl I ever loved (*he pours himself another drink*) and he'd better look after you and treat you like the lady you are—(*he holds up the glass to look at it, and then drinks from the bottle instead*)—or he'll have me to answer for ... with ... to ... (*he has another drink*) ... I'm not a man to be trifled at ... to ... with ...
Harriet I'll convey your message.
Richard I want some mice.
Harriet Mice? What do you want mice for?
Richard I want some mice for my drink.
Harriet Oh, ice.
Richard That's what I said.
Harriet But it's brandy.
Richard (*loudly*) I don't care I want some mice!
Harriet (*shushing him*) All right. I'll get some but then you really must go.
Richard Yes.

Harriet goes into the kitchen

Richard carries on drinking

Anne comes out of the bathroom

Gordon Good bath?
Anne Terrific. I'm glowing with Badedas.
Gordon Well don't glow too much, I don't think I can trust myself.

Richard gets up and goes to the sofa table shelf to look for another bottle. His back is to the bedroom door

Anne Now, now. You've got two ladies already. Remember two's company, three's a crowd. I'm off to bed.
Gordon Plenty of room in here.
Anne Good, you can spread yourself out. (*She opens the door, sees Richard, slams it and comes back in*)
Gordon Changed your mind?
Anne Yes ... I mean no ...

Richard knocks on the bedroom door

I mean yes! (*She leaps into bed*)
Gordon Who's that?
Richard I want a word with you.

Anne (*hastily*) Tell him he can't come in. (*She dives under the sheets*)
Gordon You can't come in.

Richard opens the door

Richard Now look here ...

*He sways backwards and forwards in the doorway. Gordon begins to sway in
unison*

Gordon Stand still ... stand still whoever you are ... Come to that, who the
    hell are you?
Richard Never mind who I am. (*He wanders to other side of bed*) I've just
    come to tell you to look after her.
Gordon Who?
Richard You know who. I thought she was mine, and then she was his and
    now she's yours.
Gordon You're drunk.
Richard Thas no excuse, you look after her.

Harriet enters the sitting-room with the ice

Harriet Where are you?
Richard In here.
Harriet Oh God, no! (*She dashes into the bedroom*) You've no right to be in
    here.
Richard I've just been telling him to look after you.
Gordon Who is he?
Harriet Be quiet.
Richard Because I love her.
Gordon Who?
Richard This lady of yours.
Harriet Be quiet.
Gordon Do you know this man?
Harriet Yes.
Gordon Well you might introduce us.
Harriet Very well. (*Pointedly*) He's a vet.
Gordon (*unconcerned*) Oh yes.
Harriet From New Zealand.
Gordon (*still unconcerned*) Really.
Harriet His name is Richard.
Gordon How do you do ... (*realizing*) Richard!

*Gordon pats the bed frantically and quickly lifts a corner of the duvet up and
shows Harriet that Anne is in the bed and then covers her up again*

Richard (*eyeing the bed*) Hang on he's got someone in bed with him.
Harriet Of course he has, it's his wife. They're very old friends of mine from
    Faversham. Gordon and Anne Wilson.
Richard Oh I do apologize, old man.
Gordon Quite all right, old boy.
Richard And may I apologize to your good wife.
Harriet No, she's asleep.

Richard (*trying to pull the bed clothes back*) I insist.
Gordon Leave those alone.
Richard But I must apologize. (*He lifts the sheets at the bottom of the bed and calls out*) Forgive me, dear lady, for disturbing your slumber.
Anne (*in a false voice*) Not at all, please go away.
Richard Not the action of a gentleman.

He flops drunk across the foot of the bed and hurts Gordon's leg

Gordon Ow!

Harriet checks that Richard is now unconscious

Harriet All right, madam, you can come out now.
Anne (*emerging*) Poor old Richard. Out like a light.
Harriet He's a damn nuisance.
Anne I expect he was feeling miserable and came looking for me.
Harriet No, he came looking for me.
Gordon You? But you belong to me.
Harriet I don't belong to anyone.
Gordon I pay your rent.
Harriet Yes, but it doesn't give you "droit de seigneur" over every floosie in the neighbourhood.
Anne Floosie?
Harriet You'd better make up your mind. Who's it going to be, me or Miss New Zealand?
Gordon You've got it all wrong.

The doorbell goes

Anne There's someone at the door.
Gordon Damn the door. Get this drunken lout off my foot.

Harriet and Anne swivel Richard round. In his stupor he cuddles up to Gordon, putting an arm over him. Gordon throws it off in horror. Richard does it again, Gordon throws it off and in doing so smells Richard's breath. He recoils in double horror, and gets off the bed

Harriet (*to Anne*) Right, now you are sleeping on the sofa. (*To Gordon*) And you, in the bath.
Gordon In the bath? But there's a drip in it.
Harriet Well there's room for one more.

Harriet pushes Gordon into the bathroom and follows him in

The doorbell rings again and Anne goes and answers it

Magda (*off*) I've come to see my husband. Mr Gordon Farrow. He's here with a broken leg.
Anne Would you mind waiting, please? (*She closes the door on Magda and comes back to the sitting-room. Calling*) Harriet . . .

Harriet enters the bedroom from the bathroom

Harriet Yes.

Anne There's a lady to see you.
Harriet (*entering the sitting-room*) Me? What about?
Anne She wants to see her husband, Mr Gordon Farrow.
Harriet *What?*
Anne He rang his wife and told her he was in a nursing home?
Harriet Which nursing home?
Anne This one.
Harriet Oh, lord. Anne, you've got to help me.
Anne Me? I'm just the neighbourhood floosie.
Harriet Well, now you're the district nurse. (*She picks up a white table napkin from the sofa table and hands it to Anne*) Put that on.
Anne (*draping the napkin across herself*) Is that all I'm wearing?
Harriet On your *head*. There's a clean overall in the kitchen. Put that on too.
Anne Yes, Matron.
Harriet And make sure it's done up.

Anne exits to the kitchen

The doorbell rings again

Harriet takes a deep breath, straightens her hair, and goes and opens the front door

She lets in Magda Farrow, an imperious lady in her forties

They come into the sitting-room

Magda I really do apologize for calling outside visiting hours, but I've been so worried ever since my husband rang and I finally managed to trace the address from the phone number. It wasn't easy, I had a frightful job with Directory Enquiries. They denied all knowledge of a nursing home in this road but I gather you must be a very recent establishment.
Harriet Recent, the paint's hardly dry.
Magda Are you the matron?
Harriet Of course.
Magda And was that one of the patients who let me in?
Harriet Good heavens, no, one of the staff. Sister Anna.
Magda It's a little unusual not to be in uniform, surely?
Harriet (*excusing herself*) Well we've just had our annual staff dinner, and Sister was going off duty, but unfortunately the night nurse hasn't arrived yet . . . so she's just going back on duty.
Magda So you're doubling up are you?
Harriet Yes, we have to, it's the demands of our profession. It's just one of those days, frantically busy.
Magda New arrivals all the time?
Harriet The doorbell never stops.

Anne enters from the kitchen. She is now wearing a smart white overall with a wristwatch pinned on it. The napkin has been fashioned into a nurse's headgear with a couple of safety pins. She looks smart and efficient

Anne Ready for duty, Matron.

Harriet gives her a look

Magda Well I must say that when my husband rang me he seemed to be a little uneasy at the treatment he was getting.

Harriet I can't understand why. I would say he'd been extremely well treated.

Magda He said it was a dreadful place.

Harriet I can assure you with the utmost sincerity his is the first complaint we've ever had.

Anne Absolutely the first.

Magda If you don't mind me saying so, it doesn't look like a nursing home. (*She moves towards the dining-room door*)

Harriet Well this is just the annexe, the main house is round the corner.

Anne We only take emergency cases in this part.

Harriet hastily picks up the whisky bottle, whilst Magda is looking into the dining-room. Anne clears the brandy bottle and glass

Magda Looks more like a private house.

Harriet (*glancing at the whisky label*) That of course was Sir Johnny's intention.

Magda Sir Johnny Who?

Harriet Sir Johnny Walker—our founder. This annexe was his private house that he left on the stipulation that nothing should be altered. He felt that the atmosphere of a private residence had therapeutic value in many cases, and was conducive to a speedier recovery. (*She puts the whisky bottle on the sofa table shelf*)

Magda And does it?

Harriet We haven't been open long enough to find out.

Magda My father was a doctor you know.

Harriet Oh really.

Magda I always found the usual hospital atmosphere rather overpowering.

Harriet Yes, all boiled cabbage and chloroform. We do our best to avoid it.

Magda There's a very pleasant perfume in here. What is it?

Anne Miss Dior.

Harriet (*quickly*) A present from a grateful patient.

Magda Let's hope my husband has cause to be equally grateful.

Harriet I'm sure he will.

Anne Yes. He's most appreciative of everything we do for him.

Magda Really.

Harriet Which in Sister's case is above and well beyond the call of duty.

Magda I gather he fell over in a shop.

Harriet Oh really, we weren't too sure where it happened.

Magda On some fish I think ... and what exactly has he done to himself?

Harriet The doctor said it's either a fracture or a very bad sprain and he ought to have it X-rayed. And of course there's the concussion.

Magda Concussion?

Harriet Spasmodic.

Magda It really is too bad. May I see him?

Anne Actually he's having a treatment at the moment, if you'd like to go into the waiting-room we'll call you as soon as he's ready. (*She indicates the dining-room*)

Magda Isn't it a little late for treatment?
Harriet We offer a twenty-four hour service here. Would you mind ? (*She indicates the dining-room*)

Magda walks to the dining-room door and opens it as:

Alec enters the sitting-room from the hall L, wearing his pyjamas and dressing-gown

Magda stays in the doorway

Alec I laid on the bed and dropped off.
Harriet Oh good.
Alec Where's my vodka?
Harriet I'll bring you some more in bed.
Magda Good heavens!
Alec (*seeing Magda*) Who the hell's this?
Harriet Never mind. (*Quietly to Anne*) Dash around and look busy.
Anne Just going to see who's popped off in geriatrics.

Anne exits to the hall L with an exaggerated busy walk

Alec What the hell's going on and why's she dressed like that?
Harriet (*sotto voce*) She's just had a bath and washed her hair.
Alec I'm going to need that vodka.
Magda Do you allow drinking to all hours?
Harriet He's a special case.
Alec And I happen to be her husband.
Magda How very unfortunate for you, Matron.
Alec Matron?
Harriet Darling, there's no tonic, go and get one out of the fridge will you?

Alec moves to kitchen

Alec (*stopping at the door*) God, this isn't your mother, is it?
Harriet No. (*Pushing him out*) Just get the tonic.

He exits

Magda This place doesn't seem to be run on very orthodox lines.
Harriet I think I should explain to you that that poor man suffers from a mental disorder.
Magda If he lies in bed all night ploughing into vodka I'm not surprised.
Harriet It's not really vodka, it's plain water but he's none the wiser.
Magda Oh I see.
Harriet We have to adopt psychology with him.
Magda It's a bit of luck he's married to you, Matron.
Harriet Good gracious me, he's not.
Magda But he said he was.
Harriet That's part of his mental illness, he only thinks I'm his wife.
Magda Why should he think that?
Harriet Well he had an accident.

Anne bustles in from the hall L with an empty wine carafe

Magda He had an accident?

Anne Yes, but it's all cleared up now.

Harriet No, Sister, I was referring to Mr Bulthorpe who thinks he's married to me.

Anne Oh him, yes, he's a very pathetic case.

Magda What sort of accident did he have?

Harriet He was riding.

Anne And fell off his mount.

Harriet Or some such thing.

Magda Oh dear.

Harriet And it left him with er . . .

Anne Sporadic amnesia?

Harriet Or some such thing.

Anne Oh, he was unconscious for days, Matron never left his bedside.

Harriet When he finally came round I was holding his hand.

Anne Or some such thing.

Harriet And he's been under the impression ever since that I'm his wife.

Magda How very difficult for you.

Harriet Only occasionally.

Magda I've never heard of a case like that before.

Anne It's quite common round here.

Magda What's it called, Matron?

Harriet Er . . . what's it called, Sister?

Anne Er . . . Polygamous . . . er . . .

Harriet Palsy.

Magda Polygamous Palsy?

Harriet I'm afraid so.

Magda And does the patient continually tremble?

Anne Yes, with anticipation.

Magda Anticipation of what?

Harriet He thinks he's got more than one.

Magda More than one what?

Harriet More than one wife.

Magda Oh, you mean like a harem.

Harriet That's it exactly.

Magda Tragic.

Harriet Very.

Magda How do you cure it?

Harriet It's not easy. But we find time heals most things. We have to humour him.

Magda Doesn't that lead you into some curious situations?

Harriet Yes it does, but our training enables us to handle the patient's psychoses.

Anne Or some such thing.

Harriet (*brusquely*) Sister, whatever you intend doing with that thing, kindly do it.

Anne I'm off to the lab. Anything I can get you?

Harriet No, but don't forget you've got to help Dr Head with his heart transplant.

Anne Right-o, Matron, I'll go and scrub up.

Anne exits to kitchen as Alec enters with the tonic

Alec Now perhaps I can have my drink?

Harriet Of course you can, sweety-pie.

Magda It'll all help to clear your mind, won't it?

Alec I beg your pardon?

Magda You're in very safe hands, I'm most impressed with the staff here, well some of them.

Alec Would someone mind telling me who this lady is?

Harriet Later, dear, later.

Alec (*bearing down on Magda*) Who are you?

Magda (*nervously*) I'm a married woman, with a husband.

Alec I'm very glad to hear it, but what are you doing here?

Magda I've come to visit him, he's here with a broken leg.

Alec He's what? How many wives has he got?

Magda (*with a nervous giggle*) Not as many as you.

Alec Not as many as me? What's going on?

Anne enters from the kitchen

Anne The fuse has blown on the life support machine.

Harriet Never mind that. I'll mend it later. Take Mrs Farrow into the waiting-room. (*She points to the dining-room*)

Anne Very well, Matron. This way, madam, please.

Magda Thank you.

Magda and Anne exit to the dining-room

Alec Who is this woman?

Harriet No-one, have your drink.

Alec Yes, but who is she? (*Pouring himself a vodka and tonic*) She said she was married to Richard.

Harriet She is.

Alec But Anne's married to him.

Harriet That's right. They both are.

Alec What?

Harriet Darling, you know I told you that Richard had that awful time in New Guinea and lost his memory.

Alec Yes?

Harriet Well, it seems that when he married Anne he forgot that he was already married to that woman.

Alec Oh, during the blank period?

Harriet Yes.

Alec And doesn't she know?

Harriet Oh, she was told, but the shock sort of unbalanced her.

Alec Oh heck, you mean she still thinks she's married to Richard, then?

Harriet Exactly, and she thinks this place is a nursing home.

Alec Why?

Harriet Well, ever since New Guinea she's had a fixation and thinks everywhere's a nursing home. It's a harmless delusion.

Alec Going to be a bit of a shock for him, isn't it, poor chap?
Harriet Could well be. So I'll have to break it to him gently. (*She goes into the bedroom*)

Alec pours himself another vodka and tonic

(*Banging on the bathroom door*) Gordon!

Gordon opens the bathroom door

Gordon What is it?
Harriet Are you feeling strong?
Gordon No. (*He hobbles in*)
Harriet Pity. Your wife's turned up.
Gordon Magda! (*He stubs his toe*) Ow! (*He jumps on to the bed*) How the hell did she know I was here?
Harriet Because like an idiot you gave her the telephone number, and she traced it.
Gordon I told her I was in a nursing home.
Harriet And that's precisely what she thinks it is.
Gordon A nursing home? We'll never get away with it.
Harriet We have so far, just keep calm and get into bed and leave it all to Matron.

Alec wanders into the bedroom

Alec How's he taken the news.
Harriet Not very well.
Alec Can't say I blame him (*He stops on seeing Richard*) Good God, who's this?

Harriet and Gordon pause

Harriet (*brightly*) Oh him!
Alec Don't tell me you hadn't noticed him?
Harriet Yes, of course we've noticed him.
Alec Well who is he?
Harriet The doctor.
Gordon He popped in to see me on his way home from a party and passed out.
Alec Is he ... ?
Gordon }
Harriet } (*together*) Yes.
Gordon As a newt.
Alec Where did you get him from?
Harriet Mummy recommended him, he's her doctor.
Alec They make a damn fine pair, don't they?
Harriet Gordon your wife will want to see you.
Gordon I suppose she will. Where is she?
Alec In the dining-room, poor woman. You don't remember much about her do you?
Gordon Not really.
Harriet I think you ought to be in the spare room, Gordon, on a single bed.

Gordon Why?

Harriet Well, we don't want her to see you lying on a double bed with the doctor.

Alec No, she's confused enough as it is poor woman. Come on, I'll give you a hand and get you into my room. (*He sits on the bed*) Hop on to my back and for God's sake think thin.

Gordon You're a real pal, Bob. I appreciate it. It's years since I had a piggyback.

They struggle out of the bedroom

Anne enters from the dining-room

Anne What's going on?

Harriet We're trying to get the patient into the spare room so that his wife can see him in privacy. Hurry up, darling.

Alec (*suddenly*) Oh my back's going!

He drops Gordon and they both scream with pain

Harriet Shut up the pair of you.

Alec leaves Gordon propped up in the middle of the room and makes for a chair. He is now bent double, and from now on he walks like Quasimodo

Gordon Don't leave me. What about my leg?

Alec Bugger your leg, it's my back.

Anne My word business is booming.

Harriet Come on, never mind him, give me a hand with this one.

Anne and Harriet help Gordon into the hall

Anne By the way, is . . . er . . . you know . . . what's it . . . is he still flat out?

Harriet Oh you mean Dr Dayton. Yes, fast asleep, it's overwork.

Anne and Harriet, either side of Gordon, exit together L

Alec groans and sits in a chair

Magda enters from the dining-room

Magda I demand to see my—— (*She stops*) Oh, it's you.

Alec Yes . . . It's my back.

Magda It's all those wives, you've been overdoing it.

Alec Eh?

Magda Don't think I'm criticizing, I mean we all have our own ideas on marriage and if some men want to have more than one wife, who am I to cast the first stone?

Alec That sounds as if you've come to terms with it then.

Magda With what?

Alec With your husband being remarried.

Magda Remarried?

Alec Very much so.

Magda Oh he's got a harem, too, has he?

Alec Only in a small way.

Magda Well we've all got to start somewhere. How many wives has he apart from me?
Alec Just the one, the sister here.
Magda Sister Anna?
Alec That's the one, yes.
Magda Goodness, that was quick work, he only came in this afternoon.
Alec That's as maybe but they're married.
Magda It's curious how all the patients here seem to be married to the staff.
Alec (*blankly*) Are they?

Richard wakes up and gradually gets off the bed

Magda You're married to Matron, aren't you?
Alec If she says so.
Magda (*as if talking to a small child*) D'you remember how long you've been here?
Alec No.
Magda But you're happy here. I mean they treat you kindly.
Alec Oh, yes.

Richard staggers in from the bedroom, holding his head

Richard Oh, I feel awful, dreadful, my head's splitting. I must have some water, where's some water?
Alec (*pointing to the kitchen*) Through there.

Richard exits to the kitchen

Magda Is that another patient?
Alec No, that's the doctor.
Magda *What?*

Harriet and Anne enter from hall L

Harriet I think you can see your husband now, Mrs Farrow.
Magda Thank you, but I'm rather worried about the doctor.
Anne What doctor?
Magda How many do you have?
Harriet Oh, several.
Magda Well this one looked as though he was drunk.
Harriet Oh, that'll be Dr Dayton.
Magda And is he drunk?
Harriet Good heavens, no, he hardly touches it, it's a nervous disability
Magda What's the cause of it?
Harriet Well, he had rather a nasty experience in ... er ...
Anne Alaska ...
Harriet With a Polar bear.
Alec That makes a change. I've never met so many people with nasty experiences.
Harriet Then go to bed, Mr Bulthorpe, before you have one.
Alec Well, all right, but how much longer will it be before you join me?
Magda What a trial it is for you, Matron.
Harriet Oh I'm used to it. I'll give him his treatment in a moment. Sister,

would you take Mrs Farrow through to her husband. He's in the
Nightingale Wing.

Anne Very good, Matron. This way, please.

Anne and Magda go to the hall

Alec You can't miss it, you'll hear them all singing.

Anne and Magda exit L

Harriet There's no need for those facetious remarks.

Alec Well I'm sorry, dear, but that pour soul's round the twist, I was trying
to jolly her up.

Harriet I wish you wouldn't, things are quite complicated enough.

Alec You're right there. I wish you'd just stop still for five minutes and tell
me what's going on. I mean half an hour ago I was lying in bed waiting for a
re-run of that night we had in Bermuda.

Harriet And you shall have it, darling, I promise you, but I've had this
problem with Anne.

Alec You made a big mistake letting her in you know. First her husband
turns up, and he's potty, then his first wife turns up and she's even pottier,
and then their doctor arrives, stoned out of his mind.

Harriet Anne's my oldest friend.

Alec I don't mind her, it's that mob of lunatics she's brought with her. (*He
rises and walks towards her bent double*)

Harriet Don't worry, angel, first thing tomorrow they all go.

Alec They better, because I do pay the rent for all this.

Harriet You'll never see them again. (*She bends down and gives Alec a kiss*)

Richard staggers in from the kitchen

Richard Must you do that in front of me?

Alec Oh, God, here's one of them back.

Richard Don't you know how it affects me?

Alec Oh yes ... I do.

Richard It tears me apart.

Alec Well don't drink the stuff.

Richard I mean Harriet!

Alec What?

Harriet Go and lie down at once, Doctor.

Richard Only if you'll come with me, I must talk to you.

Harriet Don't be outrageous, behave yourself.

Richard But there's something I must tell you, something you must know.
(*He puts an arm round Harriet*)

Alec Go easy, Doctor, you could get yourself struck off.

Richard I'm not a doctor, I'm a vet.

Alec A vet?

Richard Yes.

Alec No wonder your mother's got a touch of the tapiocas if he's been
treating her.

Harriet Do belt up, darling.

Richard (*taking Harriet's hand*) Oh, Harriet, Harriet.

Harriet Doctor, behave yourself, this is my fiancé Alec.

Richard Oh, that's the last straw. Then there's no hope for me. Oh I feel awful, in fact I feel terrible. Where's the bathroom?

Harriet Through the bedroom there ... straight ahead.

Richard Straight ahead—right.

Richard totters to the bedroom and, instead of going round the bed, crawls straight over it and exits to the bathroom

Alec Come on, Harriet, what's been going on between you and this vet?

Harriet Nothing, I swear it.

Alec Has he ever examined you?

Harriet Certainly not.

Alec You're sure?

Harriet He's Mummy's doctor not mine.

Alec He's a vet for God's sake.

Harriet It'll come as a dreadful shock to her. She thinks the world of him.

Magda enters from the hall L

Magda I've seen my husband, he'd like a cup of coffee.

Alec I wouldn't mind a cup myself.

Harriet Could you make it, darling?

Alec Must I?

Harriet I'm so busy. Please. Pretty please. (*She kisses him*)

Alec Oh, all right.

Alec exits to the kitchen, still bent double with his arms hanging down

Magda You really do have to humour him, don't you?

Harriet Up to a point.

Magda It must be difficult knowing at what point to stop.

Harriet I've had a great deal of experience over the years.

Magda And the same goes for the sister I imagine.

Harriet Yes, she's a good worker.

Magda She's certainly working wonders with my husband. She's trying massage.

Harriet Oh, is she? I'd better just pop in and supervise.

Richard enters from the bathroom and walks towards the bedroom door

Magda I admire the way you keep your eye on everything.

Harriet One has to. Things can so easily get out of hand. Excuse me.

Magda Of course.

Harriet exits to the hall L

Magda sits down as Richard straightens his tie

Richard (*reaching the bedroom door*) Now pull yourself together. Don't forget, you're a vet. (*He comes into the sitting-room and crosses to the kitchen door without seeing Magda*)

Magda (*to Richard*) Ah, feeling better?

Richard No, not entirely, who are you, madam?

Magda (*coyly*) Do you remember the last patient you had?
Richard Vaguely.
Magda Well, that's my Gordon.
Richard Gordon? Not that Aberdeen Terrier with the warts.
Magda (*worriedly*) I don't quite follow you.
Richard Or was he the German Shepherd that hurt his leg?
Magda He's hurt his leg, but he's not a shepherd, he's in advertising.
Richard Oh, the one that does the dog food commercial on television?
Magda I've no idea, they may do. What's your opinion, could it be a
    fracture?
Richard No, a bad sprain.
Magda It was a fish you know.
Richard Fish?
Magda Yes.
Richard Oh that guppy with fin rot.
Magda No, it was a halibut.
Richard Halibut?
Magda Yes, he trod on it.
Richard Oh. Well bring it round tomorrow and I'll have a look at it.
Magda I don't think you'll learn very much by looking at the halibut. It's my
    husband. I think we're at cross purposes.
Richard I think it's quite possible.
Magda And it couldn't have happened on a worse day. A dinner party for
    fourteen, utter chaos.

The doorbell rings

    My husband was going to get home early to help me, but in the end I had to
    cancel the whole thing. And it's my birthday.
Richard (*blankly*) Many happy returns.
Magda Thank you.

The doorbell rings again

    Did you hear that?
Richard Yes, you said "thank you".
Magda No, the bell.
Richard Oh.
Magda I wonder if they heard it. (*Calling*) Matron! Sister! I think they're
    rather busy with my husband. Perhaps you'd better answer it. Could be a
    new patient for you.
Richard (*bemused*) Oh, all right. (*He goes and opens the front door*)

    *Mildred Bulthorpe rushes past him and into the sitting-room. She has a fox
    fur thrown over her shoulders. She is a middle-aged Yorkshire lady and
    somewhat furious*

Richard follows her in

Mildred Where is he then?
Magda Who?
Mildred My husband. (*She strides round the flat looking through the doors
    and flings her fox fur on the sofa table*)

Magda I'm afraid I can't help you.

Mildred I think you can. I've had Mr Bulthorpe tailed by a detective agency and they say he comes to visit here, and if I'm not mistaken I'd say you were the reason for it, you hussy.

Magda Madam, I don't know who you are but this happens to be a nursing home.

Mildred Rubbish.

Magda If you don't believe me ask him.

Richard looks over his shoulder to see who they are talking to

Richard I pass. (*He then sinks to his knees at the table behind the sofa and, noticing the fox fur, picks it up tenderly and strokes it*) Oh, poor little fellow ... it's too late. (*He slowly sinks out of sight behind the table*)

Magda I assure you it's true. I'm here visiting my husband. He was admitted this afternoon with a suspected fracture.

Mildred I haven't travelled all the way down from Grimsby to be stuffed with a load of codswallop.

Harriet enters from the hall L

Harriet I'm sorry to have kept you waiting, Mrs Farrow. (*She stops on seeing Mildred*) Who's this?

Mildred I'm Mrs Bulthorpe and who might you be?

Harriet I'm—I'm ...

Magda This is Matron.

Harriet Matron, of course.

Mildred Matron?

Magda She's in charge of the nursing home.

Anne enters, with her accustomed briskness, from the hall L

Anne (*announcing important news*) Dr Head's half-way through the heart transplant.

Harriet Oh, splendid, Sister. Is there anything he needs?

Anne Only a donor.

Magda A donor?

Harriet No, no, a doughnut. He's an American we keep him going on doughnuts and coffee.

Anne Or tea and crumpet.

Harriet (*acidly*) Thank you, Sister, keep us posted, and do stay in the operating theatre. You'll upset the doctor if he sees you in here. (*Indicating Richard*) He's very overloaded.

Richard staggers to his feet

Anne Don't worry, Matron, when he's in that condition he can't see anyone.

Anne exits to the hall L

Harriet guides Richard into a chair

Harriet Can I help you, Mrs Bulthorpe?

Mildred Just tell me why my husband comes here, because he does you know. I've had him tailed.

Harriet For treatment, madam.
Mildred Why? What's wrong with him?

Alec enters from the kitchen with a cup of coffee

Alec I've managed to make a ... (*He sees Mildred*) Good God! Mildred? (*He jolts himself and his back locks*)
Mildred (*fuming*) Well?
Alec It's my wife!
Magda Another one. Fascinating.
Mildred What's the matter with you?
Alec It's my back.
Richard (*getting up, taking a cup of coffee*) Is this for me, old man?
Alec Is it hell!
Richard Yes, it's agony. (*He sits down and dozes off again*)
Mildred (*sarcastically*) And how often are you having this treatment, dear?
Harriet Whenever he can. You see he's bent.
Mildred Bent?
Magda You mustn't think this mental disturbance of his will be permanent.
Mildred What do you know about it then?
Magda I was discussing his case with Matron.
Mildred How dare you discuss my husband's condition, I want to see a doctor.
Magda (*pointing to Richard*) There he is.
Harriet Don't disturb him he's worn out. Mrs Farrow, will you please go and sit with your husband?
Magda Very well. (*To Mildred, as she goes*) He's got an imaginary harem you know.

Magda exits through the hall L

Mildred Who's got an imaginary harem?
Harriet (*pointing to the hall*) Her husband.
Mildred What?
Alec Don't worry, love, she's a bit touched. Her husband was got at by savages in New Zealand or New Guinea or Newmarket or somewhere.
Mildred You're rambling, Alec.
Alec It's the pain in my back.
Mildred Why couldn't you tell me you were coming here?
Harriet It's the treatment. It's a little unorthodox.
Mildred Does it involve manipulation?
Harriet That's part of it. Along with phrenology and acupuncture.
Mildred It's quackery. It shouldn't be allowed.
Alec That's the reason I didn't dare tell you. You'd only have sneered at me and said I was wasting our money.
Mildred So you are. And is that supposed to be the doctor in charge? (*She goes over to Richard*)
Alec Don't wake him.
Harriet He's meditating. He goes in for spirit healing.
Mildred (*leaning over him*) By the smell of it, he's treating himself.

Anne enters from the hall L

Anne (*announcing*) Dr Heart's finished his head transplant.

Harriet just looks at her

Sorry, I think it's the wrong way round.

Harriet (*pulling Anne to the bedroom*) Could I have a word with you in private, Sister. (*In the doorway, hissing at her*) Don't overdo it.

Anne You said to keep it looking busy.

Harriet And believable. Don't go raving mad.

Anne Why not? Everyone else is. Who's that woman?

Harriet Alec's wife.

Anne Oh, how jolly for you.

Harriet (*coming out of the bedroom*) Mrs Bulthorpe may I introduce you to my colleague, Sister Anna.

Mildred Good evening, Sister. Are you the person who's been treating my husband?

Anne Yes, and Matron of course.

Mildred Sticking needles in him?

Anne Injections, yes.

Harriet No, she means the acupuncture, Sister.

Anne Oh that, yes of course.

Mildred Well it hasn't done him much good he's seized up.

Alec I haven't had it yet this evening.

Mildred Well, I'd like to watch it.

Harriet No, that's very unorthodox even for us. Take him to the treatment room, Sister.

Alec (*in pain*) No, please, leave me be, it's too painful.

Mildred Give it to him here.

Harriet Here?

Anne I'm afraid all the needles are being used at the moment.

Mildred (*opening her bag*) How about an ordinary darning needle?

Harriet I haven't got an ordinary darning needle.

Mildred I have.

Alec Stop interfering Mildred.

Mildred (*taking a needle from a pack*) Here we are, Sister. Brand new, I only bought them today for my tapestry.

Harriet We're an acupuncture clinic, madam, not the Royal School of Needlework.

Mildred A needle's a needle. Get on with it.

Harriet Very well. It's your husband.

Alec Hang on, hang on!

Harriet All right, Sister, if she insists on a demonstration give her one.

Anne As you wish, Matron.

She takes the needle from Mildred and goes behind Alec, who is bent over the back of a chair

Mildred Well, what are you waiting for?

Anne Er ... for your husband to remove his trousers.
Alec You'll wait a bloody long time then!
Harriet Give it to me, Nurse. (*She makes a couple of nasal Chinese sounds more appropriate to Kung Fu, then loudly*) Ah-So!

She rams the needle into Alec's backside. He yelps and straightens up like lightning.

Alec *Ah!* ... It's worked ... It's better ... me back's in place again. It's a miracle.
Mildred Well I must say it seems to work.
Harriet Never fails.
Richard (*having woken up*) Are we having a party?
Mildred You're drunk.
Harriet Go back to sleep.

He does so

Mildred Well, you're all right now, so I can drive you back home.
Alec Tonight?
Mildred Of course. Go along and get your things together.
Alec (*hastily*) Yes, dear. But what about the rest of my treatments?
Mildred If it's doing you good, you'd better come back whenever you need it.
Alec (*delightedly*) Oh, thank you, dear.

Alec exits to the hall L

Harriet A very wise decision, Mrs Bulthorpe, if I may say so.

Magda enters from the hall L with Gordon who is now dressed

Magda I'm taking my husband home now, he seems fit enough to travel.
Harriet He's not completely cured.
Magda When would you like to see him again?
Harriet I'll just look in my appointment book (*She picks up her diary*)
Gordon I could make it on Friday afternoon.
Harriet Then Friday it shall be. (*Writing*) "Eggs—actly four-thirty."
Gordon Thank you, Matron. Thank you, Sister.
Anne It's been a pleasure.

Alec enters from the hall L, fully dressed

Alec All right if we're going, let's go. Come along, Mother.
Gordon Good Lord. Mother. I was wondering who you were. Mother—of course. Jolly nice to meet you after all this time. I should have recognized you, but come to think of it you don't look terribly like Harriet, do you?
Magda (*puzzled*) What?

Harriet makes a wild signal to him, shaking her head

Gordon (*hastily*) Ah, but there's no reason why you should. I mean my mother didn't look a bit like me. She didn't look like my father, either. In fact, to see them together you'd never have guessed they were married. But they were, or so I've been led to believe. (*He pauses*) Well, next time you're in church don't forget to say a little prayer for all of us sick people, will you?

There is a pause while everybody looks at everybody else, trying to work out the situation

Richard And you think I'm drunk?
Magda Gordon, what are you talking about?
Gordon (*at a loss*) Er ...
Harriet It's the concussion ...
Gordon Yes, concussion. Terrible thing. It makes you concussed ... I've got amnesia you know.
Magda Amnesia? When did that start?
Gordon I really can't remember.

Gordon, with a final knowing glance at Harriet, exits through the front door, followed by Magda

Mildred We won't hang about, we've got a long drive.
Harriet Goodbye, Mrs Bulthorpe.
Alec Bye, Matron.
Harriet Goodbye, sir. See you again soon I hope.
Alec You've been very kind. I don't know what I'd ever do without you. It's been a pleasure and privilege and next time——
Mildred Oh do shut up, Alec. I expect Matron wants to get to her bed.
Alec (*with a wink*) So do I.

Mildred and Alec exit through the front door

Harriet and Anne flop into chairs

Harriet I shouldn't really be talking to you, but thank you for saving my bacon.
Anne What a night.
Harriet Just some of the hazards of being a kept woman.
Anne I think I'll stick to marriage. Even to him. (*To Richard*) Come on, Tiddles, beddy-byes.
Richard (*realizing it's Anne*) Anne, what are you doing here?
Harriet She's come back to you, angel face, all is forgiven.

Anne and Harriet lift him together and help him into the bedroom

Richard It's all too late, Anne, I'm moving in with Harriet.
Harriet }
Anne } (*together*) Oh no you're not!
Richard Ladies, please. Don't fight over me. Perhaps you could share me between you.
Harriet Bags she has the first twenty years. I'll go and get the champagne.

Harriet goes into the kitchen

Anne Come along, Casanova, it's all been too much for you, have a nice lie down.

She pulls back the duvet and helps him into bed

Richard Why are you being so nice to me?
Anne I've no idea, just force of habit.
Richard I'm an awful husband.
Anne I know.
Richard I don't deserve you.
Anne No, you don't.
Richard I don't deserve Harriet either.
Anne Oh, I don't know ... perhaps you do.
Richard Oh, thank you.

Anne gets into bed and Richard puts his arms round her

*Harriet enters with a tray containing three glasses of champagne. She goes
into the bedroom and shuts the door*

Harriet Here we are. Let's drink to marriage.
Anne Yes, he'll have to, he can't take it sober.

They drink. Harriet gets into bed the other side of Richard

Richard I'm as sober as a judge, and a pretty good judge at that.

*He starts to sing: "If you were the only girls in the world", and the two ladies
join in. The three of them are singing happily*

Mildred enters through the front door and goes to the sitting-room

Mildred I forgot my—(*seeing her fur behind the sofa*)—Oh there it is. (*She
picks it up and turns to go but her attention is caught by the sound through the
bedroom door. She opens it and is amazed*) Matron!

They stop singing

Harriet (*brightly*) It's quite all right, we're having a staff meeting ...

Mildred acknowledges the fact with a slightly apologetic wave and exits

CURTAIN

FURNITURE AND PROPERTY LIST

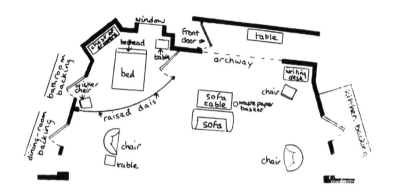

ACT I

SCENE 1

On stage: **BEDROOM**

Double bed. *On it:* sheet, bolster, 2 pillows, duvet (turned down at UL end and slightly ruffled)

Bedhead shelf. *On it:* alarm clock, telephone, diary and pen, radio

Bedside table. *On it:* table lamp

Gilt wicker chair. *On it:* **Gordon**'s jacket

Chest of drawers. *In top drawer:* handkerchief (for **Alec**), *In lower drawer:* small jewel box (for **Gordon**)

Window curtains open

Bathroom door open

Bedroom door open

SITTING-ROOM

Chair DR

Small table

Sofa. *On it:* 2 cushions

Sofa table. *On it:* telephone, full ashtray. *On shelf underneath:* glass and water carafe on tray, 2 brandy glasses, 2 sherry glasses, 3 tumblers, half sherry bottle, almost empty vodka bottle, full bottle of brandy, full bottle of tonic water

Wastepaper basket

Writing desk. *On it:* notepad and pen, spike with bills, **Gordon**'s briefcase containing papers, cheque book and pen, **Harriet**'s handbag, books

Desk chair

Chair DL

Dining-room door closed

HALL
Hall table. *On it:* vase of flowers. *Above it:* mirror
Front door closed

Off stage: Breakfast tray containing 2 coffee cups and saucers, coffee pot, filled milk
      jug, plate of toast (**Harriet**)
      Vase of flowers (**Harriet**)

Personal: **Gordon:** wristwatch

SCENE 2
Strike: **Gordon's** briefcase from hall

Off stage: Jacket with cheque book in pocket (**Alec**)

SCENE 3
Set: **Gordon's** briefcase by hall table
      Gordon's jacket on wicker chair in bedroom

Off stage: Small suitcase containing négligé (**Anne**)
      Plastic carrier bag (**Alec**)
      Tea tray with 3 cups and saucers, pot of tea, filled milk jug, filled sugar
        bowl, teaspoons (**Harriet**)
      Bandage and safety pin (**Anne**)
      Glass with ice and slice of lemon (**Anne**)
      Tray with boiled egg in egg cup, plate of bread and butter, spoon (**Anne**)
      Bottle of vodka (**Alec**)

Personal: **Harriet:** wristwatch
      Alec: keys
      Gordon: keys

ACT II

Strike: **FROM SITTING-ROOM**
      All used glasses
      All bottles to go under sofa table
      Tea tray, cups, saucers etc.
      Harriet's handbag from desk

      FROM BEDROOM
      Tray with boiled egg etc.
      Gordon's sock and shoe
      Used glass

Set: **SITTING-ROOM**
      White table napkin on sofa table
      Harriet's diary and pen from bedhead shelf to sofa table

      BEDROOM
      Small suitcase from sitting-room to side of bedside table
      Alec's pyjamas and dressing-gown in top drawer of chest of drawers

Check: Bedroom door open
      All other doors closed

Key For Two

Off stage: Bag and container with two hamburgers **(Anne)**
Bottle of Johnny Walker whisky wrapped in tissue paper **(Richard)**
Empty wine carafe **(Anne)**
Bottle of tonic water **(Alec)**
Cup of coffee **(Alec)**
Tray with 3 glasses of champagne **(Harriet)**

Personal: **Harriet:** handbag
Alec: key
Magda: handbag
Anne: watch
Mildred: handbag containing pack of needles, fox-fur

LIGHTING PLOT

Practical fittings required: wall brackets in sitting-room, bedside lamp, pendant light in hall

Interior. The same scene throughout

ACT I SCENE 1. Morning
To open: general overall lighting with bright morning sunlight through bedroom window
No cues

ACT I SCENE 2. Morning
To open: general overall lighting with bright morning sunlight through bedroom window

Cue 1	**Alec** exits	(Page 8)
	Black-out	

ACT I SCENE 3. Late afternoon
To open: late afternoon effect through bedroom window with general overall lighting

Cue 2	**Harriet** switches on bedside lamp	(Page 21)
	Snap on bedside lamp and covering spot	

ACT II. Night
To open: all practicals on, night effect through bedroom window
No cues

EFFECTS PLOT

ACT I

Cue 1   Curtain falls to end Scene 1   (Page 5)
          Loud alarm clock ring. Continue until **Harriet** *switches it off at
             opening to* Scene 2

Cue 2   **Alec** exits to bathroom   (Page 6)
          Phone rings

Cue 3   **Gordon** goes to hall and picks up briefcase   (Page 9)
          Doorbell

Cue 4   **Harriet:** "Now off you go."   (Page 9)
          Doorbell

Cue 5   **Anne:** "... wasting my time in New Zealand."   (Page 15)
          Loud crash from kitchen

ACT II

Cue 6   **Harriet:** "You're the only man in my life."   (Page 33)
          Doorbell

Cue 7   **Harriet** goes into sitting-room, shutting bedroom door   (Page 33)
          Doorbell

Cue 8   **Gordon:** "You've got it all wrong."   (Page 37)
          Doorbell

Cue 9   **Harriet** and **Gordon** exit to bathroom   (Page 37)
          Doorbell

Cue 10   **Anne** exits to kitchen   (Page 38)
          Doorbell

Cue 11   **Magda:** "... utter chaos."   (Page 48)
          Doorbell

Cue 12   **Magda:** "Thank you."   (Page 48)
          Doorbell

Lightning Source UK Ltd.
Milton Keynes UK
UKHW010332260119
336250UK00007B/149/P

9 780573 112584